ON THE WAY

A (Relatively) Brief Summary of
and Relational Commentary on
The Owner's Manual

Volume I
Prototypes

or

In the Beginning

by

Larry Mudd

E&R

PUBLISHERS OF O.G AUTHOR GENIUSES

Published by E&R Publishers
New York, NY, USA

An imprint of MillsoCo Publishing, USA
www.EandR.pub

Scripture quotations, unless otherwise noted, are taken from the Holy Bible, New International Version®, NIV®. Copyright © 1973, 1978, 1984, 2011 by Biblica, Inc.® Used by permission of Zondervan. All rights reserved worldwide. www.Zondervan.com. The "NIV" and "New International Version" are trademarks registered in the United States Patent and Trademark Office by Biblica, Inc.®

Scripture quotations marked NRSV are from the New Revised Standard Version of the Bible, copyright © 1989 by the Division of Christian Education of the National Council of Churches in the USA, and are used by permission.

ISBN: 9781945674877 (Hardcover)
ISBN: 9781945674884 (Softcover)
ISBN: 9781945674891 (Ebook)
ISBN: 9781945674907 (Audiobook)

Library of Congress Control Number: 2023952726

Printed in the United States of America
22 23 24 25 26 27 LSC 10 9 8 7 6 5 4 3 2 1

For Jacob

Thus says the LORD:
"Stand at the crossroad, and look;
and ask for the ancient paths,
where the good way lies;
and walk in it,
and find rest for your souls."

Jeremiah 6:16
NRSV

TABLE OF CONTENTS

A NOTE FROM THE AUTHORS

Dear Reader:

We Are very much looking forward to this time with you, and really want to make the most of it. To that end, We have two recommendations for you from the outset.

First, please do read all the footnotes, especially the ones that have more than a handful of numbers in them. The use of what is certain to be more footnotes than you generally encounter is one of the ways We've tried to make this more of a conversation than a lecture.

Also, and though We will certainly say so as Our journey commences and progresses, We also very highly and strongly recommend with regard to all the footnotes with number codes in them that you follow along with a decent copy of the ancient writings of Hebrew Scripture. You may call that a Tanakh, an Old Testament, a First Testament, or That Dusty Thing on the Bookshelf next to the outdated encyclopediae; or you may need to pick up a fresh copy right now.[1] We do think it better to have a physical copy if at all possible rather than just a virtual one, as there will be a far greater sense of journey as We move through a physical volume together; however, better to use an app than not follow along at all.

We promise that these efforts will be worth the investment.

Kindest regards,
The Authors

---

[1] We will largely be using what is commonly known as the New International Version® (NIV®) of the Bible (unless otherwise indicated), but just about any flavor will work. Do have one handy, though.

FOREWORD

For many people, the greatest challenge with the idea of God is that God, as they understand him, seems uncaring, aloof, antiseptic, detached, impersonal, standoffish, and even forbidding.

Holy? Oh, for sure! They've heard many times about the transcendence of God. The ineffable one to whom the angels cry out, "Holy, holy, holy."

Larry Mudd, writing with the heart of a pastor, is helping us understand that this holy God is both transcendent and immanent. He's a loving father who cares about his creation. He comes near; he listens; he empathizes; he heals.

One of my family's close connections to Larry is that he was—for many years—the worship minister at a New York City church where our son and daughter-in-law attend. Because of that, I think of the tradition of hymns.

The vast majority of them affirm the "otherness" of God. God is "a bulwark never failing." Thankfully, we serve a God who isn't just a buddy—full of the foibles that beset us. This God is majestic and righteous.

But there were always other hymns, too: those that intimated the nearness of God and his unending love.

My God and I go in the field together,
We walk and talk as good friends should and do.
We clasp our hands, our voices ring with laughter;
My God and I walk through the meadow's hue.
We clasp our hands, our voices ring with laughter,
My God and I walk through the meadow's hue.

Or (from a song an older friend of mine who died recently sang every morning):

He walks with me, and he talks with me;
And he tells me I am his own.

And the joy we share as we tarry there,
None other has ever known.

As we read this journey through the story of scripture, let us remember that while God is indeed transcendent, ineffable, and mysterious, he is not uncaring and hard to love. God cares *for* us—just as he cares for the birds in the air and the flowers in the field. And he cares *about* us, working constantly in ways of love and mercy for our redemption, our healing, and our well-being.

~Mike Cope—Pepperdine University, pastor, and author of five books, including 2011's *Megan's Secrets.*

Chapter 1
Through the Habitat Glass

Finally. There you are. I've really been looking forward to this. I've actually been working on getting you and Me[1] to this moment for quite a while. By the time We're through, I think you'll be able to see that. I've been trying to get your attention for a long time – actually, for your whole life – and at last, you've begun to take notice. Hallelu-Me! Right now there are some things going on that are making you think or wonder about Me a bit more – or they're about to – and this is the perfect time for you to read this. Whether you're on an investigative mission, indulging your curiosity, or simply picking up something you won't blow through in a few days, it's no accident you noticed this book on the shelf or web, or that your friend gave it to you at this particular time. I know a thing or two about timing. That's not to say you had no choice in the matter – you always have a choice. I just help things along with a nudge here and there so the choice seems more or less obvious at the right time.

Here at the outset, you and I are going to have to work together to build a vocabulary of sorts. We've got some pretty big concepts to work through, and I really want to avoid anything that smells of hollow cliché or off-putting jargon. The first problem to tackle is how you refer to and think of Me. That's pretty much the whole point of the book, so let Us just get it out there on the table. And like everything concerning Me, figuring this out is a bit of a challenge but worth the effort.

For a good 4,000 years, folks have been using "Father" to address Me, which is fine – I told them to do it. But it's just not that simple. I mean, a rose by any other name might smell as sweet to Bill Shakespeare, but names are powerfully important and carry with them layers of meaning, association, and impact.

---

[1] We will reverentially capitalize all pronouns and nouns that refer directly to Us as We go along.

Now, no one is more aware than I Am[2] that as you sit there (or stand there, or lie there…), you are living and perceiving life from inside an environment that significantly shapes your view and experience of reality. Slowly reread that last sentence, please. Good. The word "environment" is certainly a good one, but We want to add an awareness of your being in it on, well, a permanent basis. Yes, you can change geographic locations, or even spend some time on the moon, but the formative role of your environment is inescapable. You cannot cross its mobile borders since you carry this entire frame of reference within you everywhere you go. And so, We're going to paint in broad strokes here and say that your environment and everything that comes along with it all the time is your personal habitat, like Wild Cat Country at the zoo but on a much bigger scale. It's just as mobile as you are, but just as inescapable as Wild Cat Country. Your habitat is the realm in which you live as you relate to and experience reality within a set boundary that involves a host of factors.

A large component of habitat is your culture. Culture isn't just what someone "gets" when they have some high-end experiences, like going to see an opera or museum. Everyone's got a culture, whether or not they know who wrote Carmen or painted The Starry Night. Culture is the fish's water: It's the world in which you live, on big and small levels. It includes your family, home, neighborhood, town, geographic region, country, probably even continent, and everything in between. The part of your culture with which you most strongly identify has a whole lot to do with what you think is good or bad, desirable or shunned. Your culture preloads assumptions in you without your even knowing it. It defines beauty and assigns value, and automatically narrows down all manner of options from an otherwise overwhelming menu of possibilities on every level.

The food menu is the easiest illustration of this factor. Dishes thought to be a tasty delicacy within one culture can cause someone from another to lose their lunch: chitterlings a/k/a "chitlins" (pig intestines), raw oysters, head cheese (if you don't know, you don't want to, trust Me), caviar, tripe (cow's stomach lining), fois gras (liver of a goose that's been force-fed corn). You get the point. Transfer the concept to pretty much everything, and you have a glimpse of how massive a role your habitat plays in your experience of life.

---

[2] Since "I Am" is My Name, it will be capitalized as well, along with its variant, "We Are," all of which We promise to get around to explaining, at least somewhat.

Most humans are so busy focusing on their own habitat, they suffer a double blindness of sorts. First, they don't realize there are other habitats out there, like the cheetahs that have no idea the rhinos even exist on the other side of the zoo. Then, to make matters even more complicated, humans don't grasp *how much they are being shaped* by their own habitat, like the gorilla that believes all trees have tires swinging from them because his does. You're a child of your habitat too, and have to work really hard to get your imagination out of your own habitat in order to look objectively at, well, anything.

So when I told humans to call Me "Father" – yes, We're back to that now – culture was one of the reasons I made that choice. I Am not actually male. Or female. I had to make one of each gender to adequately articulate My image on earth, but that's getting a bit ahead of Ourselves. Hear this: I transcend gender. (Actually, I transcend everything.) However, there is no real example of a genderless sentient being within your experience. (Several human languages even assign gender to inanimate objects, as many of you grew up knowing.) However, I had to pick something in order to give humanity a better chance of understanding and relating to Me, so I went with "Father" because it fit best with your culture.[3]

I Am not a man, but for Our purposes, I'm going to stay on the male side of the tracks. Like it or not, it still meshes with your habitat standards, and I've got the momentum of the last 4,000 years headed that way too. How you address Me is ultimately and obviously your choice, but I strongly recommend something with a relational bent to it. Constantly referring to Me as "God" keeps you feeling like I Am pretty distant, which is why I've chosen "Father." So, if a plain "Father" works, fine. It's likely, though, that that feels a little starched, so if you can work your way towards something a little more relaxed, that would be better. Hebrews call their male parents "Abba," with "Daddy" being its closest equivalent in English, but there's more to it than that. The thought of calling Me "Daddy" probably makes you feel a little too juvenile anyway, which I can appreciate.[4] Why not try "Papa" on for size? You might like it. Or choose something from outside your habitat and adopt Me as your Abba.[5] Try to call Me **some**thing that

---

[3] Unfortunately, this left room for "Mother Earth" to have her moment in the sun (which is Mine, by the way) and for "Mother Nature" to make those cheesy margarine commercials back in the 70's.

[4] Of course, from My perspective you are a juvenile. No offense.

[5] That's a nice tall "ah" sound at the beginning, as in "car" (unless you're from New England). However, if you can't get the Swedish pop quartet out of your head, "Abba" isn't a good fit for you.

helps Me feel closer than a million miles away. I Am right here, and ready to further My relationship with you.

We immediately run into trouble, though, because your male parent, no matter what you called him, totally blew it in more ways than one, and you remember this clearly. (The same could be said of your female parent too, though in many cases not quite so dramatically.) I Am not here to talk about parenting per se, but the topic is unavoidable since I'm essentially everybody's Daddy. I'm also aware that We'd have to go into much too long a tangent if I were to address every variance of parenting and/or family situation you're experiencing, so just go along with My having to speak in general terms. *If* you have or had a dad as part of your life, don't project his shortcomings onto Me. 99 times out of 100, your dad was doing his best the only way he knew how, but every human dad is broken, some more (or *way* more) than others. Hear this: I Am not them. I Am not broken.

I Am on your side. Really. It may not have felt like your dad was, but believe Me when I say I've got your back. Because, regardless of your human dad's feelings about you, I in fact Am crazy about you. That's right. You. And regardless of whether your dad was there for you, I Am here, and I'm not going anywhere.

Think about it. What does a dad do? At least in a best-case scenario? Gives life to you, protects you from harm, and gives you what you need to grow – all when you can't take care of yourself. In those early days, he gets excited at every little milestone, from talking to walking to finally pooping in the toilet. (After all those diapers, that *is* exciting!) He teaches you about life and the world, the things that are good and the things that are harmful. He helps you have fun and plays with you, provides opportunities for rest and joy. He takes you to cool places to discover more about the world. He encourages you to discover your own strengths and aptitudes, then empowers you to become strong in who you are, equipping you to face the world for the day you'll step out on your own into the adventure of life in a new way. I Am the dad you always dreamed of, all the good things you see in human dads to an exponential degree. Who's your Daddy? I Am!

So for now, let's intentionally anthropomorphize Me and make use of some of your habitat-generated assumptions about good parenting. We'll paint Me as the Father of all fathers, the Überdad, in the hopes of taking your relationship with Me a little further along The Way. I'd say I'd like for us to get to know one another, but that would be a half-truth. You see, I already know you better than you know yourself, dear friend. So what I really want from this time We're spending together here is for you to get to know Me *and* for you to accept the fact that I do know everything about you – the good, bad, ugly, and unspeakable – and I'm *still* crazy about you.

Now, lots of people talk a lot about Me. You could say I'm a hot topic of conversation, even though everybody knows you're not supposed to talk about religion and politics in polite[6] company. Actually, I'm not here to talk about religion. There are plenty of other people doing that. They mean well, but there's a whole slew of folks out there telling the story of religion who think and proclaim that that story is My story. Not quite, at least not in the sense of what most people mean when they use the word "religion" these days. I Am not a system. I Am the living God, creator and sustainer of all that is, and the One Whose love for you knows no bounds. If I Am truly at the heart of your religion, that's one thing. If your religion has reduced Me to a grumpy caricature, as many have, that's an entirely different matter. As a result, many of you have been driven away from Me because of "religion" without ever getting a chance to truly hear My side of the story, so one of Our challenges is the misinformation you've heard about Me over the years.

Another challenge will consistently be the whole habitat thing. A bird's-eye view is supposed to be best, seen from a lofty perspective that takes in the larger picture. Well, I see a whole lot better than any bird, and I Am the only one with a God's-eye point of view. It's not even possible for Me to share it with you: You can't get there from here! By design even at this very moment you are taking in information and forming your understanding about Me within your personal, unique frame of reference; your point of view; and your habitat. Plus, We're going to be talking about other people and how I've related to them in other times and other habitats that were not like yours at all.

In order to help you work on your habitat lens awareness throughout this journey, We will be making a concerted effort to experience and process the various texts headed your way in as close to their original intent as possible. We Are not going to be connecting stories in the opening chapters with later writings or events until We all get to those later entries chronologically, something that fits your habitat's penchant for timelines, but challenges its know-it-all-iness. Even though every one of you knows that Moses

---

[6] Ever notice how "politics" and "polite" are spelled so alike yet experienced as complete opposites?

is coming, We're not going to mention him[7] until he does. We may draw attention to this or that promise that points to his coming, but will not spoil things by saying, "Which, of course, is talking about Moses, who will get here in a few centuries," etc. I Am not telling you to forget everything you know; far from it. As you attempt to walk as firmly as possible in the shoes of the people with whom I Am dealing in the texts' instant circumstances, you may discover that you know more than you thought you did. You may also discover that a lot of your assumptions are based more on your habitat than on what We say in the Scriptures.

Just knowing about that feature of difference is half the solution, though. It's a lot easier for you to get this bit than it was for your parents. Of course, I haven't changed. That's one of My features: I Am the same – yesterday, today, and tomorrow. This doesn't mean I never change My mind. I do. When in doubt, confusion, and at all other times, think this: There has never been nor will there ever be a time when you cannot trust Me. I haven't changed, but your habitat's view of Me and My story sure have. The human race itself, as We shall be pointing out along The Way, has certainly changed over the years: and so My dealings with them/you have appropriately shifted as well. That's another sentence to reread right there.

Now, I'm not going to bandy about the latest pop-philosophical jargon to describe what's recently happened in your habitat with regard to its over-all outlook. I'll just say this: It wasn't that long ago that people believed that truth existed. Objective, we-can-all-agree-on, yes-this-surely-is-the-truth truth. Now, you might expect Me to think those were the good old days, because today's subjectivity – where something is "true" simply because you as an individual feel and/or experience it as "truth" – doesn't seem at first to lend itself to helping people find and follow Me. It seems to yield a popcorn of plurality in which I Am just another choice on an expanding menu.

It's no surprise, then, that those who still hold on to the old structure of rigid thinking pretty much panic in the face of today's subjectivity and wonder how anyone will ever find Me in the morass of individual experience being trotted out as truth these days. Don't panic, friends. I can handle it. I created experience, remember? And let Me say that plenty of those "objective" folks who laid down the law in My Name did more harm than good because they weren't pointing people toward Me – they were pointing them

---

[7]   Except for now. No way around it.

toward their system and habitat. If you want, I'll sum it up for you: Yes, objective truth exists, *but* it is experienced subjectively by each individual.

But let's not talk like that anymore. It's not that I don't like large, theoretical words. There's a time and place for them, but for now I'd rather go after a much cozier feeling (which is My subjective objective!), and stop talking about other people for now. This isn't about them. It's about Me and you. It's just you and Me, kid, and I'm not here to lay down the law. I'm here to tell you My story as simply as I can, and by the time We're finished, I hope you'll want to be a part of it and get On The Way. Or that you'll be really juiced about being part of it if you're *already* On The Way! For now, though, let Me just say that I Am really glad you're here.

Chapter 2

My Book: The Owner's Manual

Something to keep in mind throughout Our journey with you is that My interaction with you – past and present – is something that leaves the ball firmly on your side of the court in terms of whether you choose to believe and follow Me On The Way. Let's sum that whole process up with the word faith. I have deliberately set things up so that you can't be forced by undeniable proof to have faith in Me. We have provided you with enough information to make an impartial decision, but not so much that you essentially have no choice in the matter. I Am always fair. Faith is a choice.

Now, I could go on for quite a while about the implications of that last sentence there, and will restrain Myself for neither the first nor last time in Our exchange with you. With regard to faith, and related to Our prior discussion of objective/subjective truth, please carry with you as We go along that little sentence: Faith is a choice. As in, something you decide, a decision you make. Faith is not an emotion. Sure, you can feel warm and fuzzy about Me all you want. However, My goal is not for you to feel "faithy" about Me; it is for you to decide to believe that I Am, and that I care deeply about you. Each and every one of you, from your scalp to your souls. There will be times when those things feel more true than others, but neither My existence nor My love for you will ever be less true simply because you feel less "faithy" due to intervening temporary circumstance. Faith is not a feeling; it is a choice, a choice We obviously want you to make in Our favor.

However, in order to be true to Ourselves and thus keep the universe intact, We must make the decision-making process as fair as possible. As such, We've intentionally limited Our contact with you. Amongst Ourselves, We call it the fair disclosure versus full disclosure doctrine. Since it's such a force in your habitat, let's go to Hollywood for a moment. Think the infinite opposite of the Wizard of Oz. I mean, if We pulled back the curtains and let everyone see

Us as We Are, it'd all be over, and the option of not believing would totally be out the window. Behind the curtain lies power, splendor, glory, and spectacular beauty beyond the wildest dreams of Hollywood's greatest special effects artists, only these things would not be and are not "effects." They. Are. As We Are. Were you to get even a momentary real look, there'd be no question about whether I Am, or whether to follow Us On The Way.

Here was one of the greatest challenges We faced early on, since popping by for a conversation as Myself wouldn't do. I'd overwhelm you with My bodacious magnificence, and you'd bow in worship, and that would be that. So in My great love for you, I Am driven by this desire to reveal Myself to you in a way that keeps your will free and clear to choose to believe Me (or not) in as impartial a setting as possible. You older folks that knew Elvis movies, think "Clambake." That's the one where he's filthy rich but pretends to be poor so that "regular" people will relate to him. It's actually a pretty good parable from your habitat for a lot of what I'm trying to get across.[1] The rich Clambake Elvis wants people to love him because of who he is as a person, not because he has a lot of money. Well, that's pretty much Our goal too; on a larger scale, of course. We want you to love Us because of Our love for you, not because We have infinite power and can control the weather.

Our fair v. full disclosure doctrine plays itself out and shifts a tiny bit in Our brief interactions with a handful of humans over the years. Each of them already had at least some faith in Me before I give them the Full(er) Yahveh[2] treatment, so even their faith isn't forced upon them. At the beginning of My story with humans – which We really Are about to finally get to – I dial down the glory and get practically homo sapien with the first couple (I had to introduce Myself, didn't I?). This is especially true in comparison with how much more of Myself I'll reveal to a small handful of prophets further on down the road.

In those very early days, the first couple and the prophets to come are at pivotal points in The Plan, so I have a lot of (muted) personal contact with them. We'll deal with a good number of those interactions as We go along. The point I'm working towards right now, though, is that We get to deal with those past crucial moments with you now because they've been written down in My book. I first interact with Adam, Eve, Abraham, et al., in conversation and life event, and We bring you into a similar interaction now

---

[1] You youngsters can order the disc online; they're not about to stream that one!
[2] No, it's not a misprint. We'll get there.

as you and I look at their stories together. We have recorded the past so you and I can process it in the present. Those pivotal points of Our interaction with select humans On The Way are preserved as accounts in My book, just waiting for you to discover the very same truths I told those earlier humans as We set the course for The Way with them.

However, none of them is perfect. Far from it; they're human. In fact, many of those people would rather not have been written about, and for good reason. Most of them don't come off looking too good at times. This particular point – how misguided, wrong, or embarrassing some of the people in it end up looking – is a double lesson. First, you can relate to them since they're often a much worse mess than you are. If We can bless and empower them, you're no problem at all.

Secondly, this continuous parade of incredibly ordinary and flawed humans through whom We craft The Way is a pretty good rebuttal to those naysayers that think My book is all made-up fiction (like there's any other kind). Any close look will show that these ancient writings do not make those who write it look all that good. I've never quite understood how that fiction theory could ever stand up. I mean, if you're going to make something up about yourself, at least paint yourself in halfway rosy colors! Don't include so many details about your colossal failures, foibles, and screw-ups, warts and all. And if you're going to make something up about *Me*, then on one hand you could do a much better job at making Me simpler to understand. On another hand, you really don't want to be making stuff up about Me for any reason. Ever.[3]

So My book – what you call the Bible – is My story with you and your race – the human one. It doesn't answer all your questions. You can't understand all the answers to all your questions, even if I were to give them to you. Besides, if you could completely understand Me, I wouldn't be much of a God, now would I? We're operating on a need-to-know basis for now, and if you still have questions when you get to the party at the end, I'll be happy to answer them all then. We'll have plenty of time to chat.

Yes, My book has answers in it, but it's not the All the Answers Book. It's also not The Big Rule Book. Sure, there are some rules in there (don't freak out – I'll get to those in a minute), but that also is not My book's primary purpose. My book is a living, breathing account of how I have interacted with people just like you from Day One, written either by them

---

[3] Irony acknowledged.

or someone to whom they told it all.[4] We have intentionally developed and caused to come into existence this record of Our interaction so that you can decide for yourself: whether those things really matter, and if so, what their implications are; whether We have truly been acting throughout history in your interests; whether We got history started in the first place; and most importantly, whether We Are calling you into something far greater than the life to which your habitat seeks to limit you.

You've got right there in your hands in either paper or bytes exactly what I want you to have in this dynamic account of Our dealings with humanity across history. Again, and in spite of what you've been told, it is not first and foremost a book of answers or rules, though it contains both. Above all other things, My book is the evolving story of Me on a journey with people. My people. As in all the people I made. You could say that I'm a people God. Relationship is at the core of Who We Are; and at the core of what We desire for and with you is the same thing: relationship. Therefore, My book is a string of narratives – or in your habitat, snapshots and screen captures – of Me acting in relationship with humans, one person at a time across time.

Now, a recurring facet to My encounters with people is that I meet them where they are, right where and when they live, and proceed to help them further On The Way – just like you and I are having Our time together right now. This expression of Us that you're reading is unique to your time and circumstance, My friend. This is meaningful to you – at least I hope you are choosing for it to be so – in large part because I Am very aware, even as I speak, of your past and of your habitat. I know you in the city, the country, or the suburbs; in a building, vehicle, or outdoors; under the covers with a hard copy; on the go out in the community with your tablet; listening while you walk the dog, do yard work, or…

Therefore, the whole concept of habitat is a result of Our meeting every-one, including you, right where they are across time, relating to each person in a way uniquely suited to their external and internal circumstance in order to give every person the best shot at getting it all.

And so, We've introduced this concept of habitat at the outset because of its important role in, well, everything. Let Us spend some time now applying the concept of habitat more specifically to My book, because habitat's influence here cannot be underestimated. Remember, your habitat is the environment

---

[4]   Even if the story was passed through more than one generation to the one who finally wrote it down.

within and *through which you perceive* and live life. It shapes your view and experience of reality, your values, and your assumptions. So here's the thing. Without intentional effort to prevent it, you'll automatically project your own habitat-based assumptions on every story in My book. This will be both a constant challenge as well as part of the adventure throughout the whole enchilada.

Yes, the people with whom I interact in the book are people just like you and the one sitting, lying, living, or snoring next to or near you. There are clearly lots of universal qualities to humans of every time. However, your habitats are always in flux, particularly so as technology has developed in recent centuries. Change is a constant factor in all of life, and always has been; and you're sitting pretty in a habitat that is radically different from every single one of them found in My book. And though they may seem to be a lot alike from your vantage point, there are lots of different habitats within My book to boot. It's not an insurmountable hurdle, by any means, but you're not even going to see the Habitat Factor as a challenge if you don't know it's there.

Now, I used the term narrative a little while ago. You already recognize that each narrative in My book takes place in its own historical, cultural setting. In each exchange I have with people, they all, like you, are assigning values and making decisions in large part because of their habitat. As We go along, then, when you look at this or that particular narrative – if you truly are trying to derive from it meaning and direction for your own life – ask yourself which parts of what I Am driving at are universal and thus something for you to personally consider. Then consider which parts might be a function of the ancient habitat in which the narrative takes place. As you think about it all, ask yourself if you're projecting any of your habitat's assumptions onto the story that may be coloring your view of it.

You are individualistic, technological, urban, democratic,[5] educated, etc., and as such may be projecting a great deal of conflicting assumptions into a vastly different ancient setting. In contrast with your own, in nearly every habitat We deal with in My book, the interplay between community and individual is far more heavily weighted toward the group as a whole. The narratives take place in settings where agriculture and rural life ground the people to the rhythms and risks of nature and My role in it; settings where the social and political structures are wildly different from yours; settings where the vast majority of people have neither the opportunity nor necessity of learning to read; and so on. These are just a few of the issues to consider.

---

[5]   In system, if not party affiliation.

If you're really excited by the Habitat Factor and want more, you can start thinking about how two or more different habitats clash with one another in a time of war.[6] Then, things get even more complicated when the war on which you're focusing happened in the past, as is so in biblical accounts. In that event, you must realize that the guy who recorded the story you're reading was probably doing so a couple generations later in his own habitat, and now you're peeking over his shoulder from your own vantage point thousands of years later, and… Whew. Lots of subjective lenses in that mix, but regardless of how many, there is still an objective, historical event front and center.

Just being aware of the lenses or filters your habitat's placed on you, though, is more than half the battle. If you feel like doing a little historical research to get a better handle on a particular story's context, that'd be great. However, you're going to be just fine if you don't become a scholar about all this. Since I'm working on things together with you from the ground up, so to speak, I just wanted to give you a little insight here at the get go before We finally crack open the book. At the very least, I hope to help you miss some of the quicksand that waylaid some of those who came before you On The Way. Remember, I'm not out to trick you, friend. I've been interacting with humanity one person at a time throughout history, partly so that I could one day interact with you. Right here, right now.

I'm using one of your habitat's forms right now precisely so I can get your attention for a few moments. I know you're busy, and that there are many, many things, people, and forces out there that are trying to get a piece of you. You may still even see Me that way. I'm okay with that, because you're still reading. If you hear Me out, I think you'll see that what I want from you and for you are not at all what you expect, and are far more meaningful than you've imagined. I can guarantee that what I have waiting for you is far more and much better than what your habitat has on its program for you today. That's why I want to call you out of and past your habitat into My story, and into the recognition that I've been a part of your story all along. Co-authoring it with you, if you will.

And speaking of writing stories together, let's get back to My book. I've described it chiefly as a string of narratives that describe and record episodes of Our interaction with humanity over the years. It's loaded with wonderful stuff: poetry, drama, comedy, and yes, commands. The rules. When it comes to rules – and to the rest of it too, in fact – think of it as an owner's manual. Yep, that's where that term has been coming from this whole time.

---

[6] The inability to account for the Habitat Factor is in fact often a primary cause for war.

An owner's manual comes with every major purchase, detailing how your car, appliance, home theatre system, even handheld mini-blender each works. The manual tells you how to make it run, how to troubleshoot problems – basically everything you need to know for your new thing to function at its optimal level, to work the way it's been designed to work. Well, friend, My book, the Bible, is essentially this for human life.

Since I'm the One who came up with you, I know in precise detail your specifications: how you're made, what your limits and capacities are, what will damage you and do you harm, what will keep you going a long time, what will hasten your decay and compromise your functioning, what will bring you safety and joy. In short, I really do know what's best for you, and have told you what'll work and what won't.

Taking an example from what's ahead that you're probably already familiar with, you may remember the part at the end of creation where I take the day off and say I want you to do the same thing on a weekly basis. This routine rest is clearly for your own good on lots of levels. You know you need it. All I have to do is ask you to honestly answer the question, "Could you use a little rest?" and the sound of your eyeballs rolling across their sockets is so pronounced your neighbors can hear it. I put that command in the Big Ten because without rest – without refreshment of your body, mind, and spirit on a rhythmic, regular basis – you will break down. You'll dry up into a coarse husk of your former self. You'll live a life of randomly reacting instead of purposefully acting. I told you to rest because it's good for you, not because I don't want you to be able to buy beer on Sundays.[7]

A few of you know what I'm talking about with regard to Sunday purchases, whether of alcohol or other things (just ask someone in Indiana). There was a time not too long ago that there were laws on the nation's (or states') books that forbade retail business sales on Sundays in order to facilitate a day of rest. But to the many who are not On The Way, the thought of not making money any day on which they could derive profit is the crime/sin. So, in most states, you can now shop till you and the sales clerks drop every day of the week.[8]

The point in this small discussion of a single instance – Our command about resting, that is – is that the "rules" you find in The Owner's Manual are not intended as buzzkills. They're there for your own good. Like when

---

[7] In this volume, the Sabbath and its rest falls on the last day of the week, also known as Saturday in your habitat. Keep reading if you don't understand the beer reference.

[8] At the time of printing, 28 states still have Sabbath-related "blue laws."

dad told you not to play in the street. A real downer, since it was so much open space to toss the ball in, right? But he had a bigger perspective and understood the danger to your life far more than you could in your limited perspective at the time. Or like Mom telling you not to play with fire when you didn't understand how to control it, much less its power and danger. Transfer the concept to grown up issues like deceit and adultery, and you get the picture.

In spite of what most of you think, though, there's a lot more narrative than rules in My book. Again – this is because I know you. You learn better from a story than from a lecture. For one thing, you enjoy it more: It engages your imagination, and a well-told story can bring you so far into it, you can imagine yourself as part of it. That's pretty much what I'm going for. Yes, there are times when We need to get down to brass tacks and spell a few things out, but most of the Bible is in story form.[9] On purpose. And the thing I want to get through, past your habitat's lenses and onto your radar is that this story is not at arm's length, and it's not entertainment (though some of it is pretty entertaining if I do say so Myself). It's not just great literature. It's the story of all humanity, of all life, and of your life. You're writing the latest chapter of this great story with your life, friend. And the beginning of your story – yes, yours – can be found in My book.

It's about time We cracked open The Owner's Manual, don't you think?

Okay. If you don't know who Julie Andrews is or you think her only accomplishment is playing Anne Hathaway's grandmother in the "old" *Princess Diaries* movies, google "Do Re Mi Julie Andrews" and listen to the song on YouTube. The rest of you hum along with Me while I quietly sing in your ear. Start with the light guitar plucks. Good. Now, "Let's start at the very beginning…"[10]

Right away, though, We Are in figurative trouble, at least in terms of explaining the beginning things in a way that makes sense to your habitat. (You can relax, though; this part really is not going to be on the test.) Okay, here We go: The very beginning doesn't actually exist, because there is no beginning. I'm pretty sure you can get your imagination back far enough to think about the beginning of time, space, and matter. The physicists have been very excited

---

[9]   And though several stories are cautionary tales about what happens when you break the rules, plenty are on the positive side of discovering life On The Way with Me.

[10]   I've always loved that song. I did some of My best work through Rodgers & Hammerstein (and Lennon & McCartney, Ariana Grande, Rihanna, Béla Fleck, Beyoncé, Dolly, Taylor Swift, and whichever artist I've gifted in your frame of reference).

and very vocal about that for a long time. That's SO not the beginning, though. It might be yours, in a way, but it's certainly not Mine. And there's the issue. I have no beginning. I have always been. That's why the human words that get closest to My Name are "I Am," (the closest English equivalent to My Hebrew name). My Name is I Am because there has never been a time that I have not been. Nor will there ever be. You think you know what "always" means, but you don't. Not really. I mean, on your best day, "always" and "forever" feel like what, really? About 10,000 years? Not that you put numbers on those words when you use them, but to non-physicists, that's about how long "forever" *feels* to you (unless you've ever tried to write a dissertation).

So, a long, long time ago – not in a galaxy far, far away, because I hadn't invented them yet – We're talking *way* before there was anything else, there was Me. And if it hasn't sunk in yet, there's more to Me than you think. Again, way more. So when I say, "There was Me," it sounds pretty boring, but it's not and it wasn't. There is only one Me, but who I Am far surpasses what you can understand. No offense, but trying to describe My existence to you is pretty much along the lines of explaining cold fusion to a child entering preschool. Actually, that would be easier. So, as you would for them, I'll simplify things as much as I can.

As We Are going to see, there's a pile of keys to understanding the whole kit and kaboodle embedded in the handful of chapters that start The Owner's Manual.[11] The very first sentence is no exception and points to probably the hardest thing for you to understand about Me. We figure We might as well put it out there up front and center with no apologies. By now you've already noticed how easily I switch back and forth in My singulars and plurals in the pronouns and related conjugations when I refer to Me and Us and what We Are up to. This all flows right in front of you from the very beginning of the ancient text:

> In the beginning God created the heavens and the earth. Now the earth was formless and empty, darkness was over the surface of the deep, and the Spirit of God was hovering over the waters.[12]

---

[11] From time to time, We'll shorten this to a chummy "TOM."

[12] Genesis 1:1–2 (NIV). If you're one of the two people looking at the NRSV, in its translators' noble effort to exactly reflect the original Hebrew text, it alone uses "a wind from God" instead, a term that quickly becomes a recognizable idiom for My Spirit in further usage and contexts. Me bless them.

Obviously, the big up-front idea is that nothing exists but what I have made; put a different way, I make everything. Now, We Are not going to parse through each phrase in here, or this would have to be a thousand volume work. We'll talk about creation soon enough. Let's just stick to talking about Me for now:[13] the part that has Us already speaking in plurals. That part where My Spirit is able to hover over the waters all by Himself without Me along for the ride. We Are going there.

Not wanting to front-load a slew of assumptions here, let Us begin with just one. You recognize the existence of spirit on a basic level. Shakespeare writes that, "In the spirit of men there is no blood,"[14] asserting a part of your existence that is separate from blood, bone and the rest of your physicality. Breaking Our instant text rule just a little bit, Solomon does the same in a much earlier context with "The human spirit can endure in sickness, but a crushed spirit who can bear?"[15] And although this is not what they're cheering about, go to a high school basketball or football game, and you'll hear "We've got spirit, yes we do!"

Well, so do I. Only, in My extremely expansive existence, I Am so very much of all that I Am, My Spirit is His own self, operating in concert with but also *separately* from Me. (You see? I told you explaining cold fusion was easier.) My Spirit is so strong and distinct, He Is a whole other person.

Try this: If you've got any background in music or science, you're likely familiar with harmonics. I'm not just talking about singing or playing "in harmony," but rather the properties of individual tones or notes (in the music habitat) or waves (in the science habitat). Although each tone or wave is experienced and perceived as a single event, it contains the resonance of other closely-related pitches, intervals or wavelengths. In an audible note, the primary tone, the fifth, and the octave are most prevalent (there's more than that, but these are strongest). So the tone or wave is one and plural at the same time. It's kind of the same with Me, although I obviously surpass this little metaphor. I Am one. At the same time, My Spirit's resonance is so strong, He Is: I Am composed of at least two distinct "resonances," plural, yet one. Think water and steam together.

What I'm trying to get at is this: Before there was time or anything else I'm about to describe, there was just Me. Big ole Me. But I wasn't by Myself, because I had Myself for company. This singular plurality is behind the Hebrew

---

[13] And no, I Am not a narcissist. He gets introduced much later.
[14] So saith Brutus in *Julius Caesar*, 2.1.175.
[15] Proverbs 18:14

word for "God" in The Owner's Manual, *ELOHIM*.[16] Just like in English where you make most nouns plural by tacking an "s" on the end, Hebrew plurals are formed with an "im" ending. And right there in the first sentence, "In the beginning," it says *ELOHIM* "created the heavens and the earth." Each one of the thirty times in Chapter One you read that God did, said, or made this or that, it's *ELOHIM* doing, saying and making. Stay with Me, now. Grammatically, it means "gods," and is used in that manner about ten percent of the time in reference to the competition. The other two thousand something other times, though, *ELOHIM* refers to Me alone, with the quiet resonance of My being an Us present every time. It's a constant reminder that the nature of Who I Am boils down to one word: relationship. Love.

Well, that would be two words – "relationship" and "love." There's more to Me than meets the eye, or the grammar. I love My Spirit, and He loves Me. Knowing each other so well, how could We not? We have been, and have been together, and can only be so, for all eternity. Get your infinity symbol out, folks, because now is when you need it. For so many years that you run out of zeros at the end of the page, We were, and We were together, loving each other and each other's company. You'd think We were bored, but We weren't: We're talking about a whole lotta love going on.

So much love, in fact, that We couldn't keep it to Ourselves. We wanted someone to love, but We were alone together. And I must say I think We came up with a brilliant solution: We would create someone We could love. Someone We could be in relationship with and care for, who could in turn care for and love Us in a level of connection far deeper than simply getting together to play pinochle on Sunday nights.

We took Our time and put a few billion years of thought into the planning stage, and came up with a real beauty of a plan. We Are big (also in Our understatements), and We think big. We plan a creation that reflects Us, with plural resonances, if you will. If We were sticking to a chronological account of things, We'd start with the phase of creation most closely associated with Spirit, but even though He is in the first sentence, Genesis starts with the physical world, so let Us begin there. It's My favorite part anyhow, and should be yours too, because I've got you in mind when We set it all in motion, bringing Us back to where We just said that *your* story starts in My book. Let's take a look.

---

[16] Hebrew has no upper-case or lower-case letters. We will fully capitalize transliterated references to Ourselves like this one (and all other Hebrew transcriptions) as a matter of course.

Chapter 3
Let's Get Cooking

If I had knuckles, I'd crack them right now, just like Bugs Bunny when he sits down at a piano. Now, I'm not going to go into how I do it all – making the physical universe, that is. You guys are fighting enough about the whole shebang as it is (this and next pun intended). I do have a couple things to say on the matter, though, as you're expecting.

First of all, I'm tired of people saying that all things physical are second rate and everyone should really be focusing on spiritual things to the exclusion of the physical. Excuse Me, but We Are not putting all Our imagination and effort into the physical realm just so you can escape it. It is My handiwork, made with a purpose, and I don't make garbage. Or mistakes. The first words out of My mouth when We Are finished putting it all together are not, "This'll really distract them from their main purpose." No! No! A thousand times, no! We say to Ourselves, "Wow, that is *great*, even if I do say so Myself!" And I do say so Myself. All the time. As they say, "It's all good." And it is. Very.

And old, as in good and old. Honestly, I would like it very much if you all would just calm down about how and when I make the physical universe. I love your curiosity, but the fights are really getting on My nerves, especially when the ones who think they're taking Our side are arguing that I'm out to trick you. Think about it. This is where the Young Earth or whatever you want to call the theory allegedly based on The Owner's Manual ultimately takes you: I made everything 6,000 years ago, give or take a century, but I must have wanted to throw you off, because I made everything to just look really, really old. I embedded fictional fossils underground. I created waves of light and radiation to travel through space and strike Earth in a way that seems to point to an origin billions of years ago, but in fact, they're fresh off the assembly line in order to pull the celestial wool over humanity's eyes. (If you've never heard of this stuff, then just thank Me and carry on.)

People, I love you. I love all of you. Really, I do. But think twice, and then think twice again before you stand up and call Me a liar and a cheat as a way to somehow defend Me, won't you? Because when you get up and tell people everything's only 6,000 years old, the only thing I can possibly be in that scenario is a trickster and a liar. (And by the way, I can defend Myself just fine.)

Of course, I'll have a great deal to say about The Owner's Manual itself as We go along together, but for now just let Me say this: It's not a science book. Nothing against science. I love it. I made it. I Am a Scientist myself, the best around. But The Owner's Manual isn't a book of formulas on How to Build a Universe. It's not a cookbook on The Art of World Making. It's a book about *Me.* The point isn't that it takes Us however long to make things. The point is that *I* make them. Nothing around you is an accident (except maybe lava lamps). Listen, those of you that believe your eyes are focusing on this text right now (an incredibly complex ability) as the result of a chain of cosmic accidents have more faith than Abraham and Moses combined.

A strong theme in My story with you (both as the human race across history and you as in you right now) is that I deal with you at habitat level – up close and personal, in ways you can relate to and understand. And I know you totally get that your habitat (urban, technology and information-driven, empirical, individual-focused, etc.) is strikingly different from *anyone's* habitat in the mid to late Bronze Age, which is when humanity comes along enough for Me to start telling My story to them.

Now, every culture worth its salt has an origin story. I love them. There's usually at least a peek of Me in there somewhere. Usually, but certainly not all the time. I'd had it with the popular Mesopotamian tale at the time, that had the physical universe come about as an accidental side effect of a war between two second-rate "gods." In this myth, matter is derived from the body parts of the dead god (who obviously loses the battle); humanity is formed in order to serve as slaves to the remaining gods.

This story was circulating thousands of years ago, and only a couple of you have heard it before now (just the nerdy ones). So why am I bringing it up – am I still sore about it or something? Nope. Way over it, thank you. The point is this: The Owner's Manual had its genesis (also intentional) within *that* habitat. So when I tell My story of creation and how I make the heavens, the earth, plants, animals, fish, people, and everything you would ever need to invent the lava lamp, I'm making points that make sense first and foremost *in that habitat.*

Those points? Intentionality and source, friend. The universe is *not* an accident: I make it on purpose. The cosmos is *not* composed of leftover dead god parts or leftover anything: I cook it all up on My own from scratch. No Universe Helper in the kitchen that day, friend. Everything that exists does so because I speak it into existence (i.e., "And God said, 'let there be light'; and there was light.").[1] You want to know where all that matter comes from for the big bang, folks? I'll tell you – I make it. Pull it out of nowhere; or rather, speak it out of nowhere, such is the power of My Word. And you? You! Unlike the old Mesopotamian account, I don't make you humans in order to have My own personal race of slaves to answer My beck and call. The absolute opposite is what is true: I make you so I can love you. And vice versa. I wish there was a less clichéd way to say it, but the plain truth is that I make you in order to have a relationship with you. That's as corny as Kansas in autumn, I know. Well, go ahead and color Me yellow.

Not an accident, made from scratch at but a word from Me with personal, compassionate intent – these are the main points in Our creation account, as intended for that early habitat I first reveal that part to. Now here you come looking through all the microscopic and telescopic lenses of your habitat, *projecting* onto the story your habitat's values and assumptions. You measure life and time in very different ways from them. The agricultural society I was revealing Myself to back then counted time by days and moons. You may think you think in billions, but those folks sure didn't. (Besides, people didn't need to start thinking about billions or trillions until their national debts got that high.)

So for the love of Me, enough about the timing of it all, already! Yes, I took some time, but good things take time, and like I said, what We have made is very good. As far as My perspective of things goes, someone a bit later along The Way will say, "A thousand years in your sight are like a day that has just gone by, or like a watch in the night."[2] Of course, they didn't think in the millions or billions yet, and that simile shouldn't become some time measurement formula for you either.[3] The point is that your view of time is significantly limited in comparison to Ours; and that Genesis isn't about time, but about Me.

---

[1] Genesis 1:3; also verses 6, 9, 14, 20, 24 and 26.
[2] Psalm 90:4, credited to Moses, whom We know We promised not to mention before his time, but We're not giving away plot, just concept.
[3] Besides, you're given two options of either a full day or only a part thereof, working the night shift.

So, yes, friend, We take Our time and really enjoy Ourselves in bringing about the size, scope, and variety of life on the physical side of the multiverse. All starting with the elegant simplicity of electron, neutron, and proton.[4] The periodic table of the elements is a symphony of design and beauty. Just look at Our favorite molecule: H_2O – the primary building block of all organic life. It's right there in the first sentence of Genesis. Did you notice? I did! Water covers a good 70% of the surface of Earth, and also comprises about 70% of all mammals. Including you. Not a coincidence. (By the way, aren't you getting thirsty?) It's used in your blood to move things around your body, in your digestive system as a base for chemical reactions, in your joints as a lubricant, in your lungs to facilitate the trading transfer of carbon dioxide for oxygen, and on your skin as sweat to cool you down. Don't get Me started on how much I love water! Past your own bodies, it's also the primary agent that forms your habitat and environment, whether it's coming from the surface or the air in some form. (And, by the way, it's the only substance you can find in all three matter states: solid, liquid and gas!) And that's just one *molecule* in this multiverse We've cooked up for you! Obviously, there's a whole lot more to look at out there.

And We love how closely you all are looking at all of it now, like the physicists measuring the 28 billion light year diameter of the visible physical universe (physicists who know there must be more past that border, but are limited and frustrated by how *slowly* light travels so they can't see farther until another billion years pass by – then they'll be able to see up to *30* billion light years across). Light, of course, figures as a prominent building block in Genesis, first as a general reality on Day One, then as the stars (including the sun and its moonface-reflected starlight) on Day Four.[5]

However, looking the direction opposite the stars – from the large view to the little – is also wonderfully rewarding, from cracking the DNA code to the 5th grade thrill of seeing your first paramecium. But you don't need any lenses to witness how thrilled We Are to embed the variety that is part of Our own nature into the natural world. Our varietal delight is woven throughout all of it as We parcel out life to every subset of vegetation,[6] fowl, fish,[7] and animal.[8]

---

[4] I know some of you are into quarks and leptons, but let's keep this user-friendly.
[5] Genesis 1:3–5 and 1:14–19, respectively.
[6] Third day – Genesis 1:11–13.
[7] Fifth day – Genesis 1:20–23 – with the flocking/swarming creatures issued together..
[8] Sixth day – Genesis 1:24–25.

Part of the wonder of it all hits you when you consider what I could have done but decided against. Surely there'd be enough variety to choose from for the evening meal if I made a hundred types of plant, tree, or creature. Or even a thousand each. Nope. That wouldn't be nearly fun enough, nor would it be any indicator of how big My imagination is. Try over eight million species, the majority of which you haven't even discovered yet. Pick any category and run the variety rabbits – all 49 breeds of them – down their holes. For instance, check out the forty something different species of a single flavor of bird – the bird of paradise – on and around New Guinea. Their wacky colors. Their wackier mating habits. Talk about an enjoyable project!

Yep, from the great blue whale to the tiniest nanobe, We flex Our imaginative muscles and paint a world of wonders. Do yourself a favor and cue up the old "Planet Earth" programs, then take a look at Our handiwork that stretches out after the concrete comes to an end. Or better yet, travel there yourself. And once you're out past the concrete and the light pollution in the night sky, check out the stars. You don't need to witness a supernova in order to see something spectacular up there. The stars sing Our praises – and you can only see your closest neighbors (once you get out of town), maybe a couple thousand at a time if you're lucky. And that's just the ones in your own galaxy. Google "James Webb Space Telescope deep field" to get a glimpse of a mere handful of the estimated hundreds of billions of *galaxies* I put out there. I'm jazzed at how much you're learning; and think about it – you guys are just getting started with this stuff. Yes, friend, there's variety from top to bottom, from big to small in everything I make. Call it a feature of My fingerprints.

And all that variety out there is praising Me in its own way. The birds get it. They sing to Me all the time. Sure, every now and then they sing to find a mate; but at 5:00 a.m. when they break into the Dawn Chorus they're not looking to mate (it's 5:00 in the morning), they're singing to Me! Practically everything I ever made (except for humans) sings to Me all the time – and I'm talking both the animate and inanimate. The waves of earth's oceans sound the steady rhythm of My heartbeat then pound the shore in stormy majesty; the leaves of a million trees rustle whispered mysteries then wail warnings of My power during high winds. The wolves howl at the moon, the insects thrum and strum and vibrate in song. Of course, none of them have the unique capacity of knowing Me the way you can, but even the simplest of them can sense that there's someOne worth singing to out there. Take a lesson from the bugs, My friend, and join the chorus.

Now, looking at creation sure does inform you of much about Me. You can tell a whole heck of a lot about an artist (or engineer, or architect, or chef, or...) by looking at their creations; likewise, you can discern a great deal about Me from taking a look at the things around you that I have made. However, you can look at all the paintings, bridges, buildings, or recipes a person has ever made and still only experience a fraction of who they are. Well then, even though My art is writ large across the canvas of infinity, if all you do is look at it, there's a lot about Me you're never going to learn. An extremely important lot at that.

Therefore, in addition to all you are able to infer about Us from what We have made, We have also provided you with The Owner's Manual (TOM) in order to reveal those things about Us (and you) not readily observable in the known universe. As you will see, The Owner's Manual is not simply a tour guide for life on earth à la Frommer or Fodor, though some have reduced it to the level of "getting the most out of your time here." As We and Our creation are complex and deserving of intense investigation, so is Our Word. As you can spend your life learning of Me and never run out of things to discover, so it is with TOM. We can (and do) interact with the youngest and simplest of children while We amaze and challenge the wisest scholars.

We put before you in TOM nothing less than a stunning work of art that speaks to the simplest and the wisest alike, accessible to all yet a challenge to the ivory-towered. Our goal in this volume is to shed just a bit of light on the simpler end of the spectrum; to take some of the intimidation of the past away and help you see that what you're holding in Our Manual really does have a good deal to say about your life that will in fact make an astonishing difference if you let it. We'll worry about the scholars another time.

And so, as We turn more fully to the text, you've got a lot to keep in mind, but don't worry, friend. I Am here and will be here across your entire journey, way past when you finish this work and move on to others. From the outset, just remember that The Owner's Manual is unique in all time, born in multiple habitats, all vastly different from your own, crafted to be universal in its application, thorough in its exploration, and divine in its inspiration.

Knowing its unique place in Our journey with humanity, I set a key for understanding a whole lot about how things are going to work right at the beginning of The Owner's Manual. At the very outset, you've got a bit of a challenge that also serves as a template for understanding how it all works.

Alright then, it's time. Time to finally break it open. We Are not going to just sit here and talk about The Manual; you are going to have to read it. You really do have to check out TOM[9] for yourself. Panic not, friend. While you're welcome to read the whole thing someday, I'm just suggesting you take a moment now to read the first couple[10] chapters of Genesis. It's okay if you use the dusty one on the bookshelf; however, if it was your grandma's, while I do appreciate the resultant sentimental connection to her, I'd prefer you find something in the language of your habitat. Search for "online Bible" and pick something with the word "New"[11] or "Contemporary" in the title. Go on. I'll wait for you.

So. You've read it, right? The first two chapters of Genesis (and thus of the entire Owner's Manual)? Okay, if you haven't, now's the time. There is no time like the present, so give yourself the gift of Us and read it already. Go.

Good. Let's think it through a bit now. Notice how everything is made and I'm taking that well-deserved rest We mentioned a while ago by the third verse of the second chapter? Okay, hold on a minute. Quick tangent here. In order to not have to say "the third verse of the second chapter" or its equivalent in the future, we'll use shorthand. The third verse of the second chapter is commonly notated by Bible-reading, -studying, and -referring folks as 2:3. This is where the term "chapter and verse" comes from, usually referring not so much to a person's impressive capacity to have memorized so much of The Owner's Manual as to their ability to condescendingly quote it at someone in a less than compassionate manner. Tsk, tsk, tsk.

As long as I'm digressing, I want to point out that the chapters and verses were not part of the original writings. Those were inserted later by folks who wanted to talk about the stories and needed a quicker way to agree on what part they were talking about than, "the part after Joseph gets thrown into the pit – about a third of the way through the scroll, I think." Well, now you can just say you want to talk about Genesis 37:25 and find the exact spot because later editors – not the original authors – went through the whole Manual and assigned chapter numbers throughout (those headings in your copy describing what comes next are from the English translators of that

---

[9] Some of you may know a Tom worth checking out, but you know what We mean.

[10] I'm one of those beings for Whom the word "couple" means "two."

[11] As noted in those tiny credits at the outset, We'll refer mostly to the New International Version translation with a dash here and there of New Revised Standard as We go along; but feel free to try a few and choose what suits you.

particular version, by the way). Wanting an even more precise locator tool, they then dropped verse numbers through each chapter.

While I understand the efficacy of this numeric system, I did not have a hand in it like I did in the writing (we're getting to that, but not quite). Normally, it's not that big a deal, but due to your habitat mindset, those divisions will quietly train you into or away from associations. The chapter and verse guys made decisions about what things belonged together in the text that may have made sense to them, but not necessarily to Us in some instances. We get an instant example of this with the very first chapter. Some scribe, probably wanting to underscore the importance of the Resting Rule, puts a chapter break in the wrong place. His first three verses (2:1–3) are really the end of Chapter 1, The Seven Day Account of Creation. Chapter 2 needs to start at 2:4, because it starts the whole story over again *from a different point of view.*

Which opens up another fine kettle of fish.[12] Now, we're going to look at some of the truths embedded in these opening narratives in a few minutes, but for the moment, let's just talk about form and general substance to view a larger point about The Owner's Manual. We've got two accounts of the same event side by side (Let Us call Genesis 1:1–2:3 Version A and 2:4–25 Version B; We Are not assigning importance levels with these letters, just acknowledging their order in TOM). Version A is highly poetic and conveys a steady rhythm and sequence while it sets things in order. Version B is told more like a story than a poem, spends time on different details, and explains some details quite a bit differently.

Just in case you nodded off during that last sentence, and in particular the last phrase of the last sentence, you may wish to go back over it. Yes, without apology, on the very first page of The Owner's Manual, I lay forth what could be called conflicting (We prefer divergent) accounts of the same event. And, despite what you may have heard, the *truth* is in the details.

For example, let's just look at one part of these divergent accounts. Let's focus on the most important bit to you, as in the part where you enter the narrative. Version A is a poetic summary. Check it out. Genesis 1:27 says I create you – both flavors of you, male and female – in My image. I put you in charge of the planet and tell you to take care of it, etc. (Yes, We're going to talk about all of that in a minute. Hold your horses, the few of you that have them.) Then look at Version B. For starters, the entire sequence seems

---

[12] By the way, I thought kettles were for tea down there. Any of you drinking fish tea?

to happen on the same day – but focus on your bit again. I make the first human, put him in the garden, have him name the animals, then finally get around to making a female out of the guy's rib.

So here at the very edge of Our journey we're faced with a beautiful dilemma that will help Us navigate On The Way. We've got accounts of the same events that describe them in vastly different ways. You can call them parallels all you want, but that won't sync them up. Now, We've already mentioned that narratives A and B are also reactions and parallels to creation accounts in other habitats contemporary to the original writer,[13] but that really doesn't change much. My Word is still telling you about the same thing in two different ways.

Here's the key to it all friends. You'll unlock the mystery of similar quandaries and quagmires with this simple question: What's the point? We've alluded to this before, but here it is again to make it clear. It's going to frustrate you, because your habitat doesn't think like this, but you've got to trust Us on this. If I've got two conflicting creation accounts side by side here at the very beginning, I must not want you to be obsessing about synthesizing a single play-by-play empirical sequence out of the two. That's intentionally impossible. These accounts are not as much about how things *happened* as they are about how things *are*. Sure, there are clues to science and history all throughout the Manual, but it is first and foremost a book about these three things: Me, you, and Our relationship. So add that to the key: What's the point of this passage with regard to what it says about God? About me? About my relationship with God?[14]

If I've told the same story a couple of different ways, it must be because there is so much to be learned from it, a double account provides the framework to examine more facets of what's going on. It's not like We employ this device willy-nilly across The Manual; but when We do, it should underscore how important the core story is. The point of multiple versions of an event is not divergent detail; it is multiple learnable lessons. So, if as you go along through TOM you find that there are two accounts that differ on how many men were killed in a battle, how many animals were killed in a plague, or how may stalls Solomon had for his horses, you can be pretty sure that the point of the account is not about those things. Look past such distractions and ask

---

[13] We'll have a peek at them in the next chapter.
[14] If you haven't started your journal about this journey, now is an excellent time. Write those questions down across the top of the inside cover. You'll need them for the rest of your life.

yourself what the main lessons of the stories are: what they say about Me, My relationship with humans in general, and My relationship with you today.

You see, The Owner's Manual is both the primer on and the product of Our relationship with you. It takes two to tango and at least three fingers to functionally hold a pen.[15] I had the good sense to get the whole thing written long before keyboards came around, otherwise TOM would be God knows (yes I do) how long. I'm sure you'll agree that Our Book is long enough as it is. I'll even throw in a Goldilocks and call it just right. In every way.

And when it comes to how I brought the Bible to be just what I wanted, you know I didn't just hand you an already-written book (habitat note: what you've got on your table, shelf, or eReader would've been a large room full of heavy scrolls when this all started). I didn't write anything down for you, with one very brief exception – the stone tablets with the Big Ten on them (I do love Cecil's version of that part). I didn't put the ink on the papyrus. People did. Don't think dictation. Think relation. The Bible is a living, breathing, dynamic force that conveys My compassion and will through the unlikely means of politics, intrigue, rebellion, romance, betrayal, and just about every other expression of humanity you care to name as I have worked with and through people in divergent circumstances over the many, many years. People just like you who trusted, even reluctantly, that when I asked them to do something, I was going to see them through it. And, just like Moses and Martin, whether or not they themselves would see the Promised Land, they were instrumental in moving The Plan forward.

I hope you can see the beauty in all of this. We sure do. So yes, there's plenty of humanity in The Owner's Manual, but always in collaboration with Us as each writer walks On The Way, some in greater measure than others, always with the lion's share of responsibility and origin coming from the strongest partner (Me again). The prophets and other writers of Scripture are carried along by Spirit as they work, yielding a masterpiece of partnership that I have breathed and humans have written down: a vibrant, living, and active force.

So, like I say at the top of the chapter, when you hold a Bible (or look at an electronic one), it is very much exactly what I want you to have in your hands. Yes, I've brought it into being through the dynamic interplay of My relationship with individual human writers and prophets across the years; but having this "human element" as part of its genesis, so to speak, in no

---

[15] Go ahead, check, so it doesn't bug you for the rest of the page.

way lessens its importance. Or its authority. On the contrary: It is in itself an example of the partnership to which I Am calling you even now.

As such, The Owner's Manual is not a take-it-or-leave-it option if you want to walk with Us On The Way. It is Our primary means of conveying pretty much all the information We think you need about Us, you, the way things are, and the way things are going to be. Therefore, The Owner's Manual carries with it not just Our version of how We'd like things to go: It carries with it Our authority. It's quite a lot like a royal decree – Me being The King and all. Granted, it's a long decree, but I've deliberately made it as user-friendly as possible, believe it or not. Hence, all the stories. We know you'd rather hear a good story than a lecture. (Sadly, this is a lesson many religious leaders still haven't learned…)

In case I haven't made it abundantly clear yet, here it is in plain English: Get your information about Me, Us, you, and Our relationship with you from The Owner's Manual. My Book. Check whatever you're hearing from others about Me with what you read in the Bible. I've intentionally given you a lot of credit in the process, knowing that once you consider everything I've made available to you, you'll be able to discern the truth. You're a lot like Me, remember? Made in Our image. So I love that you want to go deep and know the reasons behind things We've said and done. There are good reasons for it all, and you'll find them in My Book. Again, sometimes all the answers are beyond your comprehension, and you'll come to the place where you just have to trust Me and go ahead and do what I ask. I Am the King, remember. It doesn't happen very often, but there'll be times I have to get out the "Because I said so" without satisfying all your questions. That'll never happen anywhere but in The Owner's Manual.

So you owe it to yourself (and to Us as a matter of fact) to pick up the living, breathing, royal-decree-carrying, just-what-I-want-you-to-have, everything-you-need-to-know, Word of Me, Owner's Manual Bible and dig in to the feast waiting for you there. It was never meant to gather dust, so let's look at some more together in the next chapter.

Before you turn the page, though, a word about context. We've already more than addressed the primary contextual issue concerning the role of habitat. There is a secondary and nearly equally important context factor within the text itself. We're about to start referring to specific statements and passages in The Owner's Manual. Every time We point to something in particular, keep that sentence's larger context within that section of writing in mind. In fact, as We go along, if I haven't already asked you to do so, take a moment to read the larger context. The larger context would be the story or section in which the passage is found (and ultimately in its context as part of the whole book). I won't belabor the importance of taking things in their proper context. All you have to do is listen to opponents' advertisements during a political campaign to know how much trouble you can cause by lifting a sentence or two out of its original context. Your style, maybe, but not Mine.

Chapter 4

Unpacking Eden

Okay. Back to Genesis and its lessons. We've talked a good bit already about creation on a few different levels. With regard to the actual process, by now it should be well-settled that I Am not a liar, and I Am not out to trick you. All that scientific physical evidence continuously piling up of My using a very gradual process to bring into being you and the world around you over the course of many, many years[1] doesn't mean The Owner's Manual is wrong about anything. It means it's about something other than what your assumed projections expect.

Look at it this way. I'm an artist, friend, and art takes time. As I said before, though, My book, and in particular the opening chapters of My book, are not an empirical survey of how and how long the process went on. They're about Me speaking all things into being from scratch in a big crescendo that climaxes with you. You! Yes, I do so in stages. We already talked about Moses equating My day with pretty much the largest number of years[2] he was able to imagine at the time. So let's all agree that I took a good deal more than 144 hours (6 days x 24 hours…) to whip up the known universe (to say nothing about the bits you *don't* know).

Suffice it to say I was bringing you along the whole time over the years from day one, cell one – nurturing and maturing you as My children. Whether *homo habilis, erectus, heidelbergensis,* or *sapiens*, I was guiding, molding, and leading the human race to reach maturity. As you'll see, and as you know from personal experience, your level of maturity as a race has been and is in constant flux, usually on the upswing, though not without significant regression

---

[1] Versus the magic wand "Poof!" method on which some (mostly) well-intentioned enthusiasts insist.
[2] Psalm 90:1-4 if you didn't look it up last time.

from time to time.[3] As I brought you along in those very early days, though, I bided My time until you came of age, what you could call a critical mass, in your maturity – intellectually, emotionally, and spiritually. I waited until you were ready and finally had the capacity to somewhat comprehend Us – at an intentionally simplified level. Of course, We're still simplifying things for you, but We *really* dialed things down back then.

And so, The Owner's Manual begins with a simple story. Well, after I create the heavens and the earth. That part isn't exactly simple, but We've covered that about as much as We're going to. Then I take dust from the ground and mold it into the first human.[4] Personally, I think that summing up the whole evolutionary process of Our bringing you to life in this way – as My molding you with My own hands from dust of the ground then breathing life into that inert matter – is nothing less than literary genius. Let that image sink in – the image of My hands molding you like clay, leaving My fingerprints all over you.

Nothing in the universe has more of My fingerprints on it than you. You are My greatest accomplishment, Our crowning achievement: an intricate, elegant, complex, uniquely irreplaceable mix of biology, chemistry, and that certain *je ne sais quoi* I call spirit (like Shakespeare, Solomon, and I talked about on page 18). You could say that the whole time I was creating the various facets of the multiverse, I was building My way up to you (with a burning love inside, at that). In fact, you're a unique intersection of two sides of the multiverse: physical and spiritual at the same time. We'll look more at the spiritual side a little later when your ancestors can think a bit more abstractly. For now, We'll just note that flora and fauna from aardvarks to zebus are strictly physical. This is not a commentary on their worth or beauty: They simply lack the capacity to straddle both physical and spiritual realities, as it were, because I gave that capacity only to you.

Even in the strictly physical realm, you also surpass the rest of creation in your cognitive abilities. No, you're not the only ones who are able to communicate, understand symbols, or perform complex group activities together. The presence of such things in the animal kingdom simply points to Our awesome design skills. When it comes to cognition, though, you are on even your worst day exponentially beyond the most clever animal, be it a primate or a porpoise. The purpose of your cognition? The capacity to relate and respond to Me.

---

[3]   Note My recent mention of your political contests.
[4]   Genesis 2:7

I therefore set you apart from all other creatures by physically breathing life solely into you in the described process of creation[5] – no other creature has that distinction. I make your distinctiveness even more explicitly clear when I say in the first account[6] that you are made in My image. I do not make this statement about man alone, as in when Adam is still hanging out by himself in the second account. I make the statement with regard to the whole human race. I create humanity in My image: male and female I create them.

In case you missed it, that's man and woman together. Get this part clear now: it takes both sides of the human coin – male and female – to adequately reflect and bear My image.[7] Even though I'm sticking to the Father metaphor, My nature is both masculine and feminine as you perceive these things, fulfilling and surpassing all your gender-associated stereotypes. I Am strong and nurturing, fierce and compassionate, courageous and protective, a fan of both baseball and ballet, the Giants *and* the Cowboys…

It takes both male and female to fully reflect My image. One of you isn't enough. It is man and woman together that produces the fullest reflection of Our image. A man and a woman living in adjacent apartments don't quite complete the picture either. Nothing against the single life, friends (in fact, I have given that to some of you as a gift, believe it or not); but it is when a man and a woman join their lives together into one that Our image is most clearly reflected by humanity.

This whole male/female adventure is one of My favorite parts (maybe yours too), so let's spend some time on this. We've been processing Genesis 1:27 already, so let's move on from there. The context for what's coming is pretty much the whole second creation account from 2:4 on, so please read from there to the end of the chapter again, and pay particular attention to 2:21–23. Ready? That's Genesis 2:4–25. Go.

Good. So now you know where they got the pithy title for that 1949 film by George Cukor starring Spencer Tracy and Katherine Hepburn. Let's take a closer look (at the Bible, not the movie). Now, keep in mind again that We had lots of options when creating you. Boy, could We talk about that for a long time! Imagine having a trunk for your nose like an elephant's, or wings, or…Specifically in this part, though, We had choices in terms of how to express deep truths about who you are.[8] In this foundational story, We

---

[5] Genesis 2:7 again.
[6] Genesis 1:26-27. We're going to be in Genesis a while..
[7] Or children, as you'll see in a moment.
[8] And since you bear Our image, Who We Are.

wanted to convey a connectedness between humans – specifically between male and female – on the deepest level possible. Too early to talk about cells, as in being connected on a cellular level – you all weren't going to find them for a very long time. So instead of going with a tiny part of Adam, We went with strength instead. What's the strongest part of your body? Your bones. So We took the strongest part of Adam to use as the starting point for his mate.

There is meaning to every detail in these stories. You get the whole point of My using the strongest material Adam has to offer as My starting point for building woman, right? This is not going to be a weaker sex. Keep thinking, now.

Let's think about bones a moment. There are lots of bones in your body: 206 in grownups. Infants have around 300 to start with, but several of them fuse over time – you can do the math. Why this rib versus the other 205 bony options? Oh, the symbolism! I love hiding it (symbolism, that is) all around the place for you to discover. Think about the possibilities: I could have started with a patch of Adam's frontal skull, and the woman would be symbolically both ahead and over him; a metatarsal from his foot, and she would be beneath him. I'm not going to go through the other 203 – you get the point. I choose the bone (still the strongest part) that was nearest his heart. A rib. Beautiful! Of course, that symbolism has meaning in your habitat where the heart, though now known to be your blood-pumper, still holds on to archaic (Greek) notions of its being the seat of emotion, in spite of knowing full well that such concepts and feelings are cranial functions. (Not to mention the fact that over the years, humans have thought the seat of emotions was located in their spleen, liver, stomach, or bowels…)

The rib is not only the bone nearest the heart – the organ that humans of every epoch have understood to be essential for being alive, whether they associated emotion with it or not – the rib is also pretty much smack dab in the middle of a person. So in contrast to the skull bone/over him or foot bone/beneath him options, with the rib as the foundation of woman, she instead will be beside man. Don't just bounce into the next paragraph yet. Let that sink in: Your mate is neither above nor beneath you, regardless of your own flavor. They are beside you, equal partners in life and relationship.

English does a good job of conveying this close relationship in your general terms for your flavors: man and woman. The Hebrew in which this passage[9] is originally written uses the word *ISH*[10] for man. His companion

---

[9]   Genesis 2:23
[10]   That's a long "e" as in "meet".

is *ISHSHA*, woman. Very similar, yet obviously different, whether you're talking about grammar, physiology, or emotional makeup. Your complementary flavors are a perfect fit for one another. There's the obvious physical suitability in your sexual union, but you fit together in other ways too. While each individual (and thus each couple combined of two individuals) is unique, I intend for you to balance each other. Strength has many faces, and is measured not only in muscle, boys. The strength of woman may be different from yours, but the fact that her spirit is more nurturing and caring than yours does not speak of weakness. Far from it. Likewise, daughter, the fact that I have streamlined man's psyche in order to act quickly in survival situations over the millennia doesn't mean he's as simple-minded as he seems to be most of the time. You don't need Me to detail your differences; however, some of you do need Me to remind you that I have created you as equals. Neither has more nor less of My favor, regard, or love. I have a special fondness for both flavors!

Speaking of flavor, let's move from metaphor to sensate experience in Our story. I make you male and female,[11] then drop you in a garden full of flavors. Variety is My middle name, friend, and it's just as evident in the edible flora out there as it is in the fauna. So far in the texts, you're still vegetarians,[12] but every vegetarian can tell you that there's a whole avalanche of flavor in the herbivore variety that rivals (or *surpasses*) the taste of charred flesh.

Think about your favorite fruit for a minute. Pear? Orange? Mango? Papaya? Definitely a habitat-driven choice. I don't care what you use as your example, just imagine one that is at the peak of ripeness, unbruised, big, and full of sweet juice. If you happen to have one in the kitchen, go grab it. Now take a bite, with either your imagination or your teeth. Let your salivary glands kick in as you think of the sweetness, the strength of the taste. Warm and round or sharp and strong? Some fruits are more intense in their flavor (My personal favorite is the raspberry, but don't tell the others), but they are all unique. Sure, one bunch of raspberries is going to taste pretty much like another bunch of raspberries, but the only way they're going to taste like garlic is if you leave them together in the fridge for a couple days. Here's the point: A great variety of flavors from delicate to powerful abound in what I have made. On multiple levels. Flavors that are a pleasure to experience.

---

[11] We Are not done with that, by the way.
[12] Genesis 1:29–30

You see, pleasure is My gift to you, friend. Think about it. I could have wired you to simply know you need to eat to survive, and trigger an instinct to eat the nearest leaves without any further ornamentation to the process. Instead, while you satisfy your need for calories and the energy they bring your body, I give you taste buds to experience flavor throughout the intake process: bitter, salty, sour, sweet. Yes, eating meets your instinct to survive, but I've also made it something to enjoy and savor. Or recoil in disgust and spit out because of disagreeable flavor, like a baby licking their first slice of fresh lemon!

Think of your favorite food, though, of its flavor. On the salty side, or sweet? Roll that flavor around in your memory for a moment. Now, compare that with a big bowl of leaves for supper. And I'm not talking about arugula or baby spinach here. I'm talking about whatever's growing in the back yard. Oak leaves? Pine needles? Grass? Get My point? I could have totally made you a folivore and had you eat nothing but leaves when you were hungry. Eating could purely have been a function of packing in some bland fuel source in order to power your body.[13] But I wanted more for you. More pleasure from the variety I have made. In fact, pleasure is one of the big reasons I embedded you with instinct. There's a few of both – instincts *and* reasons for them.

Instincts are an important part of you: They're all gifts from Me, and they're even part of My plan to reach Our ultimate goal. Instinct, your common denominator with the animal kingdom, is an efficient way to have you get what you need without having to think too abstractly about it. Food, shelter, safety, rest – the stuff of your individual survival. One way or another, I've made you to feel deeply unsettled – physically, emotionally, or both – until these needs are met. And I love the way I've designed you to feel pleasure in the fulfillment process. As We just explored, I love the look on your face when you're really, really hungry and then bite into something tasty and delicious. The way your eyes roll back in your head and you moan at the flavor of a fresh, hot cinnamon roll. Or the great rush of relief and peace that overtakes you when your head finally hits the pillow after hours of toil.

And let Me just say that another thing you should be noticing and savoring is how wonderful it feels to fall into bed when you're really exhausted, as your tired muscles can finally uncoil and relax in waves of settling calm.

---

[13] Consider the variety in the diets of koalas and pandas. Totally could've made you that way too, kid.

That euphoric feeling of peace washes over you, and the wrinkles smooth away off your brow…well, at least some of the wrinkles. I love watching you fall asleep. If you're a parent, you know exactly what I mean. And no matter how old you are, when you go to sleep tonight, I'll be there watching you. Not in a creepy way, but like a mommy or daddy watching their little boy or girl loosen their grip on a stuffed animal, breathe deeply and steadily, and drift into dreams. I almost wish I could get tired so I could see what it feels like…I know what it means to be at rest,[14] but I never need or get to sleep. Which is fine. Since nighttime washes across the planet in an endless cycle, I have to stay awake so I don't miss anyone's bedtime: I get so much pleasure from the look of tranquility that washes over you every night with the relief of sleep. Sometimes it's My favorite part of your day.

Okay. Your instincts for sleep and food, shelter, safety, and the like ensure your *individual* survival. Once those are covered, I've instilled second-tier instincts to kick in that ensure your survival as a race. And you know what I'm talking about, so let's talk about sex. Like your other instincts, it's My gift to you. Really. Right there in The Owner's Manual. I know you know how "Be fruitful and multiply"[15] works, but like everything else in TOM's opening paragraphs, there's a great deal going on in that simple imperative that is so much more important than where some of your minds go at first.

Unlike your other instincts, this one reaches far more levels than one, and goes deeper than most of you think. Just like I talked about the whole food, flavor and pleasure thing, I want you to enjoy this part of your life, to savor it. Once again – and think hard about this as I say it – I could have built you to only come together sexually when it was time to get some offspring going to help out with all the work around the farm, and even then could have made it a rather perfunctory, pleasureless activity with far fewer nerve endings involved – something more along the lines of eating pine needles. But I didn't.

Now, in addition to the pleasure of their fulfillment, there are some other, less pleasant general similarities in the exercise of all of your instinct-driven appetites. At the extreme ends of every one of your instincts lies significant peril and harm. Too little of the essentials, and you die. Too much of them, and you'll experience irreparable damage or even death. You can call it over-indulgence all you want if that makes you feel better, but when your

---

[14] Genesis 2:1–3
[15] Genesis 1:28

over-indulgence crosses the line and begins to harm you or others, We call it sin. We want you and everyone else to be safe and healthy.

Because it feels so good to satisfy them, your appetites can also be co-opted by an even deeper drive within you, a spiritual one. We will certainly speak more about it soon enough, but for now let Us simply say that you are essentially equipped with a profound spiritual need to find Me. Sometimes, these signals get crossed with your physical appetites, and you try to fill your spiritual emptiness with physical things like food, sex, possessions, etc. Since, however, these physical things are not able to fill your spiritual emptiness, things can get ugly, and the consequences start to roll.

Now, your other instincts are individually acted, and if you overdo it, you're the one who pays for it by tipping the scales too high from gluttony,[16] or losing your job for sleeping in too many mornings. Eventually, though, you'll cross over past "just" hurting yourself into harming others. When it comes to over-indulging your sexuality and the damage it does to you, someone else immediately suffers consequence, even if you think you're not hurting anyone with your online viewing habits. Some of those consequences are staggering: devastating relational breakdown, sex trafficking and slavery, sexually transmitted disease, discarded unwanted children,... Need I continue? Suffice it to say that when one of My gifts to you – be it hunger and thirst or the needs for rest and coupling – when a gift is not used as it is intended to be used, bad things happen.

On an even deeper level, though, go back to the part where I was talking about Us before time, and how at the core of Who We Are is relationship. We Are joined and entwined on a level that once again transcends full description and understanding. While nothing on earth approaches what you could call the supernatural intimacy We have with one another, We have given you the capacity (there's that word again) to experience a little slice of heaven when you come together in human sexual relationship.

Your sexual drive is intended to move you beyond yourself into relationship with another human. Given your selfish tendencies, unless I put something in you to drive you towards another human, you'd have likely lived out your days alone in order to have complete control over your environment. You'd have been reduced to a destiny determined by the location or position of toilet seats, toothpaste caps, and cheese slicers.

---

[16] You don't need Me to remind you that this is also a path to an early grave.

Sooner or later for most, however, there's a stirring deep within you that moves you to connect with another person and become their mate.[17]

My intention is for you to strongly associate with your mate the sexual bliss you experience together in order to bind you closer together in as tight a relationship as is available on earth, the nearest mirror to Our closeness together. When the ecstasy you experience together is associated with your mate, you are bound more closely to them, and vice versa. This close bond is another part of being made in Our image, as at Our core We Are in intimate relationship with One Another. Of course, not in the way that you are, but on another plane entirely. However, your joining lives together as mates mirrors this best on earth and operates on every level – physical, emotional, spiritual – and is brought about by entering into a covenant[18] together.

And so, even as sexual union is part of this, not just any coupling will do; a one-night stand doesn't reflect My image, nor does a let's-see-if-this-works-for-a-while approach. No, a man and woman do not become one flesh[19] by simply fitting their parts or their furniture together. Becoming one flesh and fully reflecting Our image results from a sacred sequence that, while it differs somewhat from one habitat to another, involves vowing to live the rest of life together in exclusive commitment to one another, then consummating that vow in sexual union. Some habitats talk more than others in making their vows, but every habitat's wedding tradition ends in bed together at the end of the day. That honeymoon night, then, is just as sacred as the ceremony. The bride and groom who have entered into verbal covenant with one another before human witnesses cross the final threshold of physical covenant and seal their vows.

Another major aspect of My design is that your coming together to form one flesh produces life. Love brings life on every level, and nowhere more clearly and beautifully than as the result of a couple's physical union. This is actually another way you bear My image – I create and sustain life on a universal scale; you do it one baby at a time.[20]

---

[17] Another entire volume could be born in order to process the shift in how many of these issues work themselves out in your habitat in ways far different from those before.

[18] Covenants will be a big part of Our journey with humanity. If it's an unfamiliar term, think of it for now as a sacred contract.

[19] Genesis 2:24

[20] Usually, that is. There've been a whole lot more multiples since you all discovered pharmacological fertility.

This is another reason for your different designs – not just a matter of plumbing and supplies, mind you, but because of the different roles you play in creating and sustaining life. I don't want to belabor this point, but it speaks to The Whole Plan. Before We're done, I'm going to have to mix My metaphors like a Cuisinart in order to help you understand the parts you can comprehend about Our ultimate goal. You're probably getting sick of My saying things like this but I'm compelled to once again mention that any human situation I put forth as an illustration is a very dim shadow of what reality is or shall be. At the same time, though, you *are* made in My image, and as such, there's a lot of this you *can* get.

So here's the caveated illustration. Let's say that this whole story, and everything I've been working for and toward, has the final goal of ending up together at the universe's most extremely spectacular, wouldn't-want-to-miss-it party. One could say that this party is costing Me everything. (It is. It has. Everything.) But to Me, to Us, it's worth it. You're worth it. And as long as I'm going to this extravagant expense, I want as many people to be there and enjoy it as possible, and there's room for everybody. So I tell you not only to "be fruitful and multiply," but for the number of people that result from your passionate covenanted encounters to be so great as to "fill the earth" with humans.[21] It's taken a while, but you're getting close; however, there were many times over the years that things didn't look so promising.[22]

Here's where other aspects of your design therefore come into play. Once again, We're painting in broad strokes here, but see if this makes sense. Lovemaking yields life, unless interruptive precautions are taken. The more you make love, the more babies you have. I know you're with Me so far. One of the primary reasons behind your "frequent frequency" desires (if you're the one who feels that way) is Our goal to bring as much life into being as possible, so that there will be as many people – each one of them conceived in sexual union (or a clinical mimic) – as many people at the ultimate (in every way) party as possible.

Just being born doesn't mean you'll make it to the party, though. Party attendance requires survival (something your habitat takes for granted when earlier ones didn't have that luxury). And you've got to find your way to The Way (which – good on you – We're all working together on right this moment). You can trust that I make sure everyone gets an invitation at some point in their life, at just the right moment.

---

[21] Genesis 1:28
[22] If this sentence puzzles you, look up "Global Thermonuclear War."

Now, in terms of physical survival, and at the risk of over-generalizing, it's apparent from Our design of conception, gestation, and birth that survival is one of the primary reasons that moms are given the gift of emotional and spiritual connection with their children. Those months of carrying new life don't just give junior time to develop physically; they provide an opportunity for deep bonding between mother and child so that once a son or daughter is born, he or she will be nurtured, protected, and thoughtfully cared for. And survive.

Obviously – and again in broad strokes, friend – We design men to be capable of conceiving more children than women, part of the "fill the earth" plan We mentioned. This is why polygamy is allowed in the early sparsely-populated days more than now when you've filled just about everywhere but Greenland with people. Since We're talking about Genesis, though, and getting things off to a decent start there at the very beginning, We design men to be able to make as many babies as possible, and to generally want to do the thing that makes them as often as possible. Of course, I had to wire them so that the connection between babies and lovemaking drops off their radar in the heat of the moment, or they'd rarely go through with the sacred act.

We won't say that women necessarily have a superior design[23] but will say that We place in them an advanced capacity for emotional and spiritual connection in addition to the physical. Pardon My speaking in generalities as certainly every single one of you is an individual unique in all time – something I know better than you do yourself – in the greatest display of variety in all creation. However, as We set life in motion, We put strong relational instinct purposefully at your core, ladies. Without you there with all the maternal gifts I've given you to guard and guide them with, those poor kids would be on a diet of who knows what at six months if their dad was taking care of them. Those broad-spectrum emotional/spiritual differences between mom and dad play out and, ideally, complement each other as your kids grow and mature.

Okay, We've gotten this far: The two archetypes of the human race are in the garden. Now, before I begin to bandy the word "archetype" about – and I'm going to – let's make sure We're all on the same page with it: "The model from which later examples are developed, or to which they conform,

---

[23] Though if I saved My best work for last, My fashioning the woman in Genesis 2:21-23 is My final act of creation…

a prototype." Don't you just hate when they define one fancy word with another fancy word? Here, then, is the definition for prototype: "An original model or pattern from which subsequent copies are made, or improved specimens developed."[24] Sounds like they mean pretty much the same thing.

Adam and Eve, then, are the archetypal prototypes for everyone that comes after them. Even the meanings of their names speak to this. In Hebrew, *ADAM* means "human;" *HAVVAH*, which is translated in English to "Eve," means "life." Their simple story is in its prominent place in the The Owner's Manual because it lays a theological foundation for your existence, exploring themes like those We've mentioned already. You're made: by Me on purpose, in Our image, to experience bountiful flavor and variety, to be in relationship with one another, to be in relationship with Me, to make plenty of babies and fill the planet…What happens next between the three of us – Adam, Eve and Me (actually four, if you count the villain) – pretty much plays out for the rest of My book.

---

[24] Lexicon Publications: Webster's Dictionary, New York, NY

Chapter 5

That Damned Tree

L et's return to what is for Our purposes here the most important arche-typal theme: choice. Remember, I have woven together in you spiritual capacity along with the beauty and diversity of physicality. As I've been emphasizing, you are unique in all the universe, both as a species and as an individual. Plus, there's more Me in you than in anything else, though still in miniature. Like the animals, you are encased in mortal flesh; unlike the animals, you are not driven solely by instinct[1] and instead have the power to choose. You have the capacity to make decisions like nothing else in the physical universe – even the glorious supernova has no power to choose its fate. You do. Since I was giving you so much power, I did not give you immortal life in the beginning. I made you mortal with the capacity to be made immortal by Spirit. We'll talk more about that in a bit, but in a nut-shell, this mortality relieves you from having to live with your bad choices for all eternity. You can thank Me later.

Those two themes – mortality and choice – are encapsulated in two symbolic trees in Eden: the Tree of Life and the Tree of the Knowledge of Good and Evil.[2] It is made clear in the archetypal tale that the humans are not immortal, and that eating fruit from the Tree of Life will make them so. In fact, they are cast out of Eden as a consequence of their sin[3] in order to prevent their ever gaining access to the Life Tree (and boy, are We going to talk more about that). Suffice it to say that the potential to gain eternal life by eating fruit from the Tree of Life underscores the *absence* of eternal life in humans on their own. You might want to let that sink in a bit, because a whole lot of folks over the years have read a whole lot of extra mojo into the

---

[1] Your years in high school excepted.
[2] Genesis 2:9.
[3] Genesis 3:22–24.

part where I breathe life up Adam's nose at the beginning.[4] That's how he becomes a *living* soul, *not* an eternal one.

I'm usually a big fan of Plato, but his ideas on the soul are wishful thinking from Our perspective. The challenge is that those ideas are so embedded in your habitat's thinking, you automatically assign an eternal soul to these human prototypes as you read, even though the text says otherwise. You even think I'm contradicting Myself by pointing out that Adam's soul is alive in Genesis 1, but not eternal. That's how deep Plato's influence has run for generations now. He's the one who came up with the idea of everyone's soul being eternal, or at least made it a popular idea.[5] Not Me. From day one in My Book, eternal life is not a given. The Tree of Life doesn't get many lines in these early chapters, but the truths its presence conveys should not be underestimated. Just because I made you with the *capacity* for eternal life doesn't mean you possess it. You'll be okay, though, friend. We have a Plan.

So let's look more fully at that word "capacity." It conveys My having created you with the *potential* to be spiritual (and eternal) on top of your hard-wired physicality. On one level, every human is a spiritual being because I have made you in My image. However, your acting spiritually or even acknowledging being spiritual is not a given. That's where your capacity to choose comes into play in a big way. You can choose to acknowledge Me or not, choose to seek and follow Me, or not. By the way, this is My primary purpose for giving you the capacity for choice: so you could choose Me. Not so much so you could choose pizza over broccoli, lumberjacks over accountants, blondes over brunettes… you get the point. The pleasure of making those choices is My gift to you as well, but My ultimate hope is not that you'll choose Beethoven over bluegrass, but that you'll choose to open your heart and your will to search for Me. We've mentioned that some already, but now it's time to roll up Our sleeves and get to the bottom of choice once and for all.

In archetypal Eden, choice is embodied in the Tree of Knowledge of Good and Evil. The humans are free to eat of any other tree in the garden – this is the only one I tell them to stay away from. At this point in time, there is only one commandment: Don't eat *this* fruit, for it will kill you.[6] It's hard to imagine a life in which there's only one mistake you can possibly make,

---

[4] Genesis 2:7.
[5] His teacher Socrates had a hand in it to be sure, but Plato's *Phaedo* puts the idea of everybody getting an eternal soul on the map.
[6] Genesis 2:15–17.

only one thing that can go wrong, only one temptation to cross your mind. But there it is, right there in Eden.[7] The first moral choice. Right smack dab in the middle of the garden. Because of what seems to be a central location (though it's not like I draw out a map of the place for you), the forbidden tree represents a kind of perpetual crossroads for the first couple, something they can easily pass by on a regular basis should they choose to do so. Then, each time they pass it, they decide whether to obey Me or not, whether they realize they're making a choice in those moments or not.[8]

It bears noting that the Knowledge of Good and Evil Tree is in the same general area as the Tree of Life, but since I haven't forbidden them to eat from the Life Tree, the Life Tree's existence hasn't come to their attention yet. The humans only know about the deadly tree because I've told them not to eat from it.

Which is a conundrum, if you think about it. Had I not told them about the dangerous tree, it may have stayed off their radar, just as the Tree of Life is not yet in their awareness. I had to warn them, though. The association between warning and awareness is the price of doing moral business in a way; there's no way around it, and no way to really wrap your mind around it fully. Since I'm both your Designer as well as your Father who loves you more than you can understand, I know best what will damage and hurt you and, because of My love for you, want to keep you from it. Since I *know* all things (not *cause* – major difference) and know what you're going to do, I have to tell you to keep away from danger. But often, just being told not to do something creates a nearly undeniable urge in you to do that very thing, or at least an urge to imagine doing it.

You know what I'm talking about. It happens with everything, from the most dangerous things (which I'm not going to mention so you don't imagine them) to the most innocuous. If I had a solar system for every time one of you touched the paint under the "wet paint" sign, either literally or metaphorically – the sign that was there to tell you to *not* touch the paint – I'd have a whole extra galaxy in My pocket. There's no way to not warn you of harmful things, though. What kind of human father doesn't tell his babies how dangerous fire is, or chasing balls into the street, or watching too much

---

[7] The simplicity of the options here is one aspect of Eden's archetypal role.

[8] While We Are certainly going to go on excursions of life application as We go along, We cannot do so in every available instance, or We'd never finish this work. However, you're certainly bright enough to see parallels in your life in this last sentence without Our pointing them out to you. Well, We just did, but in the future, feel free to do so without Our suggesting it.

of whatever today's most insipid children's program is? If I didn't warn you of danger, I wouldn't be much of a Father. Avoid Barney, Life in the Dreamhouse, and their current equivalents at all costs.

And yes, I can hear your shouting thoughts, at least in most of you: Why put the forbidden tree there in the first place? Why give humanity access to the knowledge of good and evil and set them up for failure? If creation was okay with only one bad choice available, wouldn't it have been fine with no bad choices? Wasn't I just asking them to eat that fruit by putting it there, knowing them as well as I did and do and all? Go ahead, pile the questions on, friend. They are very good questions, and I'm glad you're asking them. I'll take a hard question over an easy answer any day of the week.

Once again, I'm going to start with a frustrating reminder that this line of questioning is going to end in mystery on the You Gotta Trust Me level. But here are a few things to chew on before We get there. First of all, a life in which no options exist would get pretty colorless, especially if you get around to eating from the Tree of Life (and you would have) and end up spending all eternity in an existence akin to that of the Care Bears or My Little Ponies or Teletubbies or whatever cloying saccharine franchise the younger set in your habitat is drawn to now. Without options, you'd be stuck in infancy. Infancy is great for infants. It's a beautiful time of life. But sooner or later, maturity comes along. At its heart, maturity is a function of making choices. Choices you can't make unless you have them available. The ability to make choices enables you to graduate out of your infancy. When people start telling you, "You're acting like an infant," it's clear you've outstayed your time there. No tree? No choice. No choice? No maturity. No maturity? No freedom.

That's the word right there, friend. Freedom. Holy cow, that one is a big, fat, hairy deal: You are free to choose. That's essentially what freedom is: the ability to make choices. The opposite of freedom - being enslaved, or jailed, under house arrest, oppressed, etc. - is all about removing your choices, taking away your options. So in order for freedom to even exist, in order for you to have a life of freedom instead of one in which every choice is programmed for you by default simply because there are no other options, those other options have to really exist. Are you with Us here? Because deep down, this is perhaps the most significant expression of Our love for you: giving you your freedom. I could have made a life for you in which there were no options other than good ones. I could have made you to be incapable of making bad choices that would damage you or others – the old robot scenario, where everything about you is programmed, including an autonomic relationship with Me. What kind of life would that be? No, instead, I made you to be free, knowing when I did so how you would exercise that freedom and rebel – like any two-year-old or teenager – and knowing I would be there for you when you got hurt because of it and came running back to Me in tears.

If you choose to come back to Me, that is. Which brings Us back full circle to the primary purpose of your ability to choose. Not to get all mushy on you, but it's all about love, friend. Go ahead and play your favorite love song in your head.[9]

In order for you to be able to love Me – or anything or anybody else for that matter – you must be able to choose to do so. Choice only exists when there's more than one way to go – more than one option to take. In the case of love, you must have a very real option to choose to *not* love Me if you are going to have the chance to truly love Me. And now is as good a time as any to remind you that before it is anything else, love is a choice, friend.

I Am choosing right now – this very instant – to love you, no matter how many reasons you may have given Me not to. (If you think you've given Me no reason to make that statement, I'm choosing to love you in spite of that little arrogance problem you don't know you have.) My love for you isn't based on your ethical performance. If parents stopped loving their children every time a child was disobedient? I love you *because* you're My child, because you're My kid I'm so proud of I want everyone to know. You may not feel lovable at times, but that doesn't mean I have ever chosen to stop loving you. One big problem, though, is that a lot of you don't know what love is. You're hooked on the feeling that love is emotion and nothing but.

Sure, emotions are a part of love, but let Me tell you, your habitat has systematically painted a highly flawed picture of love to the point that love is portrayed as strictly a function of your glands. Part of the problem is your language: You use "love" for too many very different feelings. Whoever's taking the English language to its next level needs to take a lesson from the Greeks. They've got three words in play where you only have "love" as an option. (You Greek scholars can skip the next page.) Most of what your habitat calls "love" is really the *eros* flavor in Greek: erotic attraction. This is more of an interplay of instinct and pheromones

---

[9] Anything but the old "Muskrat Love," please. Oh, great. Now you're thinking of it anyhow. If you don't know it, do yourself a favor and don't look it up.

than anything else. It's got its place, which we talked about already, but I'm really hoping this is not what you're sending in My direction. Keep it in the species, folks.

Chummy affection for your pals, co-workers, or siblings (on a good day) gets its own word in Greek too. You look across the baby shower or poker table and say, "I love you guys," where the Greeks would say "I *phileo* you guys." If you'd rather be in *Phila*delphia with W.C. Fields, it's named such as the City of Brotherly Love, based on Greek's *phileo* sentiment for comrades, peers, and brothers and sisters who've gotten over the trauma of spending their childhood together. I suppose you're welcome to send some of this My way, but I'm not exactly going to reach the "buddy" level with you, and I Am certainly not your peer. No offense.

The third Greek word that hits the nail of love I'm talking about right on the head is *agape*. *Agape* is love that chooses, friend. It's what We've got for you, dear one. If you're married or considering it, you're going to need some *agape* if you're going to hang in there together when gravity kicks in and metabolism drops off in the spouse to whom *eros* led you. *Agape* is an act of will, not necessarily in spite of appearances, but based on things far more significant than appearance. It is love that sees the deep value of another person, that chooses to commit to be and remain in relationship with someone regardless of circumstance. *Agape* is love that builds the happy memories to cherish, then works together through chapters of challenging struggle to an even deeper, more mature relationship that has weathered the storms and knows it won't be abandoned at the first sign of trouble. That's Me all over, kid. I Am not going anywhere.

But you can. You can choose to ignore Me and pretend I'm not here. You can rail against or put down the people who are doing their best to follow Me, turn your back on Me, whatever. It's your choice. It really is. I give it to you freely. That's how much I love you. Can you get that? Look at it through your parenting lenses if you've got some. This really is huge, friend. Because of all the freedom I'm extending you – freedom to ignore Me, refuse Me, or deny I even exist – should you *choose* to *agape* Me, it is really going to mean something. To both you *and* Us. It's what I want more than anything. But instead of forcing you into it, I put the archetypal Tree of Choice (a/k/a Knowledge of Good and Evil) in the garden. Your prototypes therefore have the freedom to choose whether to follow Me, and you have the power to opt out in your life. All so that the only way you will (or can) love and follow Me is because you *want* to. It's your choice.

Take the Tree of Knowledge of Good and Evil out of the garden, and it's all gone: choice, maturity, freedom, love. Yes, these things will cost Us dearly, and you as well, but We love you too much to sentence you to an existence without them. And what's going to happen at My Plan's completion is only going to be possible if those who are in attendance (including you, I'm hoping) have freely chosen to be there. In a way, you could say that by placing the Choice Tree in the garden at the outset of time, We Are extending Our invitation to the Final Banquet from the very beginning.

I really, really, really want you to be a part of it all, to make the choice that gets your RSVP in the guest list, something We'll eventually call the Book of Life. Like I've said, I'm not going to force you to do anything you don't want or choose to do. I have given you a little help, though. You see, part of your dual physical/spiritual citizenship includes a yearning that goes deeper than the cellular level: an aching need to get to Me, a primal spiritual desire to find your completion in Me. Though there are many themes in the opening of Genesis, the deepest one in there is that your original design is for you to be in direct contact – face to face – with Me. Heaven and Earth are together for a short, precious time there at the beginning, and I walk together with humans side by side and talk with them like old friends, or like close family that's not been wrecked by dysfunction (yet).

Because of its foundational importance, let's examine this from multiple angles. The simplest is this: When humans are torn apart from Us as a consequence of sin (yes, We'll get to that too), and can no longer be together as you were designed, that's when the proverbial hole gets torn in your heart. Part of you is left behind. But it's more than just an emptiness. It's like I've built a homing device deep inside you that, once awakened, produces a restlessness in your spirit until you've found Mine. You can choose to ignore it, or respond to it.

As We mentioned in the last chapter, because this spiritual heart hole feels so big, no matter how you try to fill it with other things – achievement, sex, possessions, relationships, drugs, acceptance, etc. – the emptiness remains. That's because the hole is shaped like Me, and only bringing Me into your life will come close to filling it on your side of heaven. One particularly bright fellow in the fourth century said, "You have made us for yourself, O Lord, and our hearts are restless until they rest in you."[10] This restlessness of heart surpasses physical instinct, but until a person's heart is awakened,

---

[10] Augustine of Hippo in his *Confessions*.

We've already noted that the spiritual restlessness of a sleeping heart is often confused with physical instinct. We'll revisit this in a moment.

First, though, We've talked a whole heck of a lot about the capacity to make a choice, but so far in our archetypal account, it seems like no one's made a choice yet. Actually, your first ancestors have made several choices already, it just doesn't seem like it. They have chosen to *not* eat from the Tree of Knowledge of Good and Evil every time they've chosen to pass by it, or every time they've chosen to take another path to the other side of the garden in order to avoid it. They may have chosen to establish habits of travel[11] that keep them away from the location of temptation.[12] The best way to succeed in dealing with temptation is to stay as far away from it as possible. Are you getting this? Why go near something that can kill you? So the archetypal couple keeps their distance for some time; not something that hits you over the head unless you look at it a while.[13]

Speaking of subtlety, enter the snake. That's all he's called in this account. As time goes on and much further on in the journey, he'll be referred to as someone else with whom We'll deal later.[14] We deliberately refrain from giving the snake any remarkable characteristics in the story (except for his ability to speak, of course). There's nothing supernatural or spiritual about this snake, other than his penchant for fostering temptation. Sometimes a snake is just a snake; sometimes it isn't.

And though there may be more to this one than meets the eye, at the text's writing, it is not time to say much else about him. You see, there was simply no way We were going to let that early habitat who's receiving this text for the first time think that any of their tales about multiple gods having their spats about this or that had any traction in reality. We've only just begun the epic of revealing, well, everything to humans. Tell people in that early habitat that the snake is a supernatural being who's disguised himself in order to wile My children away from Me, and those initial folks would've thought, "Hey, that sounds like the rivalry between Tiamat and Marduk," or make some other connection that would lead them astray and away from

---

[11] This would be a good time to extrapolate this concept in the general direction of the temptation in your life.

[12] Oh, I can hear the rabbis and preachers latching onto that phrase! Beware the location of temptation! Amen.

[13] Yes, there's lots of subtlety in My Book, if I do say so Myself, enough to go after your whole lifetime and never reach the end of discovering fresh gems.

[14] Those few tidbits won't appear until much later in TOM.

Our final destination. This is the same driving concept that'll keep a good deal else about Who We Are under wraps a good while. We're revealing truth in manageable doses, working at square one toward as much revelation as your species can handle. We're at as simple a starting point as We can get, and across the years will add layers as you move toward the point of full maturity. Or what will eventually have to pass for it.

So the snake strikes up a conversation with the woman in Genesis 3. Read it if you haven't lately. Its archetypal importance is right up there on the top shelf. The snake chats with the woman (poor gal doesn't have her name yet at this point), and what does he use for an icebreaker? Nice weather *again*? Seen the new zebra babies? Some sunset last night, huh? Nope. Straight for the divine jugular: "God's not letting you eat any fruit from any tree in the garden, right?" Basically, "God doesn't let you do anything, does He?" What a twerp. Totally untrue. Couldn't be more untrue, as a matter of fact. But that's how he works, friend, so take note: negativity and exaggeration. Sound like anyone you know?

His first goal is to get your eyes off all the practically limitless positive things you *can* do that are *good* for you, and get your eyes on the negative to make you feel like you're missing something.[15] Then he piles on misrepresentation and overstatement to make the situation look like an extreme emergency requiring immediate (damaging) action. You're looking at the birth of hyperbole, right here in the mouth of the snake.

Of course, the woman knows better – she knows the snake's assertion that I've told them to eat no fruit in the garden at all is an out and out lie. He actually words it as a question, so he's not even technically lying, just making a preposterous query. Obviously, he's not trying to get information from the woman. He wants to draw her into an interaction with him, into a conversation through which he can whisper a few suggestions. (You're tracking with this and applying it, right? If it wasn't so important to do so, I wouldn't keep reminding you.) Well, it turns out, the woman has spent some time thinking about what I told the humans not to do. After all, she is human, and paint didn't have to exist yet in order for her to be subject to Wet Paint Syndrome. However, instead of thinking about how to break the one rule, it sounds like she's actually been thinking about how to *avoid* the forbidden fruit instead, which makes My heart glad on one level, but still presents a problem. You can tell her focus has been on avoidance and not indulgence when she says

---

[15] And so, you have now met the author of FOMO.

she's not supposed to even touch it, or she'll die. That bit about not touching it was a conclusion that she and/or Adam reached on their own – I never told them not to touch it, just not to eat it.

Not to make too big a deal out of this, but this little addition on the woman's part to not touch the tree/fruit speaks volumes. In a classic playout of Wet Paint Syndrome, it seems that she and Adam have been spending a good deal of time focused on Our command to not eat from the Choice Tree. This keeps them thinking about what they're not supposed to do, thinking about and focusing on the very thing that will do them irreparable harm.[16] As long as they are concentrating on what is forbidden, even if it's in an attempt to avoid the illicit, they are on temptation's playing field. Better would be a focus on something entirely other, replacing awareness of bad options with an exploration of all the other infinite good choice options out there instead, whether We Are talking about Eden or Edmonton.

But by engaging in conversation with the snake, the woman has opened herself up to him. He is a dark genius when it comes to turn of phrase, and does his best worst work distorting My words, adding just a twist of negativity. Whereas I tell Adam that if he eats the fruit from the forbidden tree, he "will surely die,"[17] the snake simply inserts the word "not" into what I say, "You will *not* surely die," says he, and all is effectively undone.[18]

Just as the first couple serves as archetypes, so does the snake. Again, his motivations are not discussed here at the outset; all you get to see is his modus operandi – centered in negativity, misrepresenting My words and intentions and the way things truly are – with the primary goal of pushing you away from Me. We intentionally speak of him as little as possible, not just to avoid Marduk/Tiamat parallels, but to deny him the attention. Let Us say simply for now that humans are not his primary target. I Am. Of course, he can't do a thing to hurt Me, so he comes after you instead. Ask any parent what upsets them more than anything else, and they'll tell you it's when somebody tries to mess with their kids. Well, you're My kids, and nothing steams Me more than when somebody tries to hurt you. Then, of course, there's the part where he is jealous of you at the same time because of the special place you have in My heart. Lucky you.

---

[16] I can and will repair some of the harm done, but it will take the rest of time to do so.
[17] Genesis 2:15–17.
[18] Genesis 3:1–3. Note that the snake similarly inserts a single negative into My abundant offer, "You are free to eat from any tree in the garden" (Genesis 2:16) in order to throw the woman off at the start of his campaign.

Snake projects his jealousy onto Me in his exchange with the woman. He makes it sound like I want all the Knowledge of Good and Evil for Myself, and have denied it to the humans so I won't have any competition in that category. This speaks to the snake's utter self-absorption and inability to think or feel beyond himself. It couldn't cross his mind that I'd say something for your own good – he had to assume My motivations worked like his.

His conversation has its desired effect. Notice that the snake never says, "you should totally try this fruit, girl. It's to die for!" He never tells her to eat – he just prolongs the conversation so that she'll linger there by the tree. And think about it. And look at it. And look at it more closely. Do you see? *It's the time spent in close proximity to danger* that wears her down. Learn your lesson, friend, and choose your steps *before* you get into sticky situations! Humanity's downfall starts when the woman lingers in the radius of danger. Yes, it's Adam's downfall as well, since he's a silent onlooker to the whole exchange, never offering a single, "Dear, don't you think we should be going?"

When they eat the forbidden fruit, as you know they're about to, it's still their choice, though. "The devil" makes no one "do it."[19] The snake is subject to the same restrictions I've placed on Myself: no forcing anyone to do anything. Decisions are left up to each individual. Yes, the snake is a smooth talker and knows how to capitalize on humans' vulnerabilities. What happens next, however, is a choice made by the humans, the last in a series of choices they've been making both immediately prior to this moment and in days before. They've trained themselves in negativity in their focus on what they're *not* to do. Then on this day, they've chosen to walk directly past the very thing that is most dangerous to them, foolishly and unnecessarily placing themselves in the vicinity of danger. Then, when a snake – a snake! – strikes up a conversation in which his first words call into question My goodness and good will for My children; they choose to stay put and listen instead of walking immediately away from the situation, *which is always an option*.[20]

Think about what's going on in these crucial moments. There's more than just listening to the snake going on here. In remaining in this perilous position and chatting, there is now occasion to take that closer look at the

---

[19] Even if their name is Flip Wilson.

[20] By that point in the sequence, walking away is a very difficult choice to make, but up until the moment of actual transgression, flight is still a genuine final course of action.

forbidden fruit, and this is the final step before falling. Examining forbidden fruit up close spurs the mind into imagining how good it must taste.[21] After all this buildup, after all the poor choices that have been made before this moment, it is but a small step to cross the threshold from temptation into transgression. In this case, first the woman eats, and then Adam takes a bite.

As I promised would happen, "the eyes of them both" are opened,[22] and they certainly do experience something they've not encountered in life up to that point, but it's far more than they bargained for. Yes, they do know good and evil in that moment. Up to that point, they have already known good: Good is all they have known. But now, by disobeying Me, they know evil, simply by crossing the line. They know evil because now they know disobedience. As a result, conscience awakens, and they feel shame and guilt at the wrong they have done. Their innocence gone, they piece together the largest leaves they can find to cover their nakedness, which was not a source of shame before but has become so now as another consequence of the choice they have made. Yes, I gave them freedom, and they have exercised it as they had every right to. Just because one is free to do something clearly doesn't make that thing a good thing to do. They have exercised their freedom, and are about to taste its price. You get to watch as the snake's goal of pushing you away from Us is reached.

I come along in the later afternoon when I usually take an archetypal walk with My two children as the cool breezes[23] are drifting through the garden. But the kids are hiding from Me, and not in the first ever game of "hide-and-go-seek." They are hiding because of their shame. Of course, shame can only mean one thing at that point, and all hell breaks loose.

Snake gets it first.[24] It's still far too early to get into cosmic judgment with this character as far as habitat setting goes, so We stick with snake value and make it clear this little fellow has permanently gotten himself on My bad side and made himself My sworn enemy and the enemy of my children. Forever.

Then I have to be the Father to My children, and the learning curve for all humankind begins in this moment. The concept of consequence begins this day. Up to that point, it was strictly theoretical, "*If* you eat that fruit, *then* you will die." Now it's personal. And merciful at the same time. Yes, death will come now – humans are cast from the garden so they'll have no

---

[21] Genesis 3:6, one of the most monumental verses in all of TOM.
[22] Genesis 3:7.
[23] Genesis 3:8.
[24] Genesis 3:14–15.

access to the Life Tree any longer[25] – but We do not immediately strike the humans down. We let them live a good while longer. What We said is true, and death will come for them someday as a consequence of sin, but in Our mercy, we put that death a good ways off. And when it comes, it will actually protect humans from what would otherwise have been an eternity of painful compounding consequence.

However, the life that's lived until then is going to be off-garden, and that life is going to be tough. Now, as you sit comfortably in your twenty-first century habitat and exercise your abstract cognitive muscles, you're able to catalogue a long list of the side-effects or consequences of this archetypal brokenness of humanity. Remember, however, that We Are starting simply on purpose, working in broad strokes here at the outset. As such, there are only a handful of additional consequences meted out here, and each gender gets their own set.

For starters (doubly), giving birth is now going to be excruciating,[26] obviously felt solely by women. Since their fall comes so swiftly, the first couple hasn't even had time to bear a child yet, so no woman will ever know a painless childbirth.[27] As a result of the fall, the woman is also cursed to endure the rule of her husband over her and the accompanying patriarchal system that will hold sway for millennia.[28]

Shifting to Adam – and I feel once again compelled to remind you of the early habitat of the recipients of this text – his universal consequence hits at the heart of living: eating. Raising food for his family will be a painful, lifelong struggle in stark contrast to the easy food picked off the ripe trees whenever hunger kicked in back in the garden. Instead of Eden's sprawling abundance instantly available at his effortless fingertips, doing what is nec- essary now to put food on the table will take nearly all Adam's energy. This obviously is felt by the whole family, and the general consequences placed on the man and the woman have universal impact on all humankind (as archetypal events have a tendency to do).

This whole time, the garden has been a symbol of living in My presence: Heaven and earth have been entwined, and We have walked side by side

---

[25] Genesis 3:22–23.

[26] Genesis 3:16.

[27] Even though your habitat often ameliorates that pain with pharmaceutical intervention.

[28] We could spend another volume on this alone, but for now will simply point out to those who so spectacularly misuse this text to justify their misogyny that this social structure is no more desired than pain in childbirth. You're free to work on lessening the impact of **both** curses.

with the man and the woman. As a consequence of their disobedience – the first sin – they can no longer be in My presence. Not to get too existential on you, but at this point, sin has rendered humanity imperfect. And I truly Am not patting Myself on the back here when I point out that I Am perfect. Look up perfection in the dictionary, there's a picture of Me. And a hot fudge sundae. So if I'm perfect, and you're not, or rather, humanity is not, then We're faced with two options. Option One: Humanity and I stay together, in which case their imperfection contaminates My perfection and the multiverse is pretty much undone. Option Two: Humanity and I part ways for all time, leaving the universe intact but you and I separated for eternity. Option Three: Humanity and I part ways for the time being, and I repair the gulf of a rift between the realities that are heaven and earth until such time as humanity can be made perfect again. You're still reading this, so guess which one We choose.

Just before they're launched from Eden into the harsher world, Adam completes his task of naming all that I have created.[29] Finally understanding in his own limited way how much is at stake in their lives, and realizing that all the life of all humanity will begin within her, Adam names his wife.[30] He honors her with the name *HAVVAH* from the Hebrew word meaning, "to live." *HAVVAH* shifts to "Eve" for you. That her being named is the last human event in the garden is fitting, as she was the last to be created, saving Our best for last and all.

My last action in the garden is another act of mercy. I make garments of animal skin for Adam and Eve[31] in order to keep them warm, protect them from sun and rain, and cover their nakedness. A final sign that a good deal of their freedom is gone. They thought they were gaining more freedom when they chose to disobey Us and eat the fruit; instead, they lost freedom in that moment. They thought they were becoming like Me; but instead they were pushing Me, pushing My love away. They thought they were getting wisdom and knowledge; instead they learned foolishness and its consequences.

Before We conclude this lively discussion, let's return to the underlying main point of this archetypal account. At its end, you are torn from Our presence, and though it takes you a while (again, you as a race, and you as an individual) to realize it's there, sooner or later that yearning kicks in

---

[29] Genesis 2:19-20
[30] Genesis 3:20
[31] Genesis 3:21

for something really important that must be missing. There's nothing broken specifically, though it feels so; it's more that, well, everything is broken. Brokenness is unavoidable. In your best moments, though, what you feel is more than this brokenness. It's that incompleteness, the restlessness Augustine talks about. You bear My image and are designed to be with Me. As such, you can only find – and will only feel – wholeness and completion in Me. That's the key that unlocks your entire existence right there, so if you're dozing off, read it again.

So keep listening to that innate homing device that's telling you to get yourself home to Me, because your primary factory setting is for direct contact with Me, direct understanding of Me as source of all the good in your life, direct worship of Me as Me. Removed from the optimal setting of My presence, your specifications cause you to seek what was lost, whether you realize it or not. You were in My presence at the beginning, and you can be at the end, so you hunger for what you had in order to find and fulfill your destiny at My side. That's right. Your destiny. Your movies have nearly ruined that word for Our purposes, but it's still the best one for the moment. Child, I Am your Father. I Am your destiny.

Chapter 6
Cain and Babel

Okay, We're not going to process every single item in The Owner's Manual. I promise. I'll leave that to you. Before We leave the first family, though, I want to chat briefly about the second-generation boys. You know them: Cain and Abel. They're the next chapter in humanity (and in Genesis). Go ahead and read Genesis 4:1–16 if you want to get the most out of the next few paragraphs. I'll wait for you.

So, if you remember what happened at the end of the last chapter in TOM, Adam and Eve had just gotten themselves kicked out of Eden – and out of all that the garden represented. According to the very next sentence in the account, what's the first thing they do? Find shelter? A food source? Well, of course, they must have done those things, but the writer gets right down to business and so do the happy couple, and "the man knew his wife Eve."[1] I know We've talked a good bit about and enough with the sex already, but your habitat has really missed the love boat in so many ways and needs some serious retooling in this area; so let Me point out two things about that cryptic statement. First, if you're reading a contemporary translation, then its editors probably have spelled things out for you with "had relations" or "made love" instead of "knew," but "knew" is what's right there in the millennia-old Hebrew text. Don't blame that one on King James, God bless him (and We did); blame Me. There's a doctoral treatise in that one word there, friend: knew. Once again, let's play the "What We didn't say" game. Didn't say "the man lay with Eve," though there will certainly be some "laying with" that goes on in further romantic episodes down the road.[2] Nor did We say "the man had sexual relations with Eve," though that term will be used as well later on in TOM. My point? It's not like there weren't other ways to describe

---

[1] Genesis 4:1, NRSV
[2] Note that there will never be the construct of "the man laid the woman."

what happened here. So Our use of the verb "to know" to describe the very first sexual intercourse of all time – as far as Our prototypical account is concerned – speaks volumes. You don't have to be an epistemologist to know that using "to know" to sum up the act of man and woman joining together (then and now) conveys that this moment transcends simple bodily function. Biblically *knowing* one another – the intimacy I've designed you to have with one another – is a connection and bond enveloping all aspects of your being: physical, intellectual, emotional and spiritual. Your habitat has stripped this amazingly sacred and profound aspect of your existence from so much of its meaning and power by reducing it to nothing but physical climax.

Second – don't worry, this is a rather quick point, though I know which of you won't like it – note that the noun "wife" is in the mix there too. Also not an accident. Prototypical sex, as in The Way it's designed to work, involves the whole person (in that body/mind/ heart/spirit combo) within a covenanted, life-committed relationship: in a very safe place where you can make yourself vulnerable to one another in the extreme without the fear of being cast aside for any reason. Let that concept sink in deep. True intimacy can only be found in the arms of someone you know is never going to leave you. Adam and Eve knew one another that way.

And thus, fulfilling its primary purpose (also underscored by Our pointing out their bedroom activities), this coming together of the first husband and wife makes them the first parents.[3] In consequentially painful[4] childbirth, Eve bears the first child: her son, Cain. Not long after, his brother Abel comes along, and you don't hear anything else about them again until they're old enough to start earning their keep by tilling the fields (Cain) and keeping the flocks (Abel).

The end of their first season in charge comes along, and these boys have learned the most important lesson of all from their parents: Everything in their lives that's good is there because of Me. They might not be in paradise any longer, but the plants they're growing are there because I made them, ditto for the sheep, ditto for those boys' own lives, health, strength, and capacity to engage in the extremely complex activities they take for granted which are part and parcel of their occupations. However incomplete it may be, this awareness of My provision of all things triggers the first recorded act of worship. No choirs. No sermons. No suits, ties, hats or gloves. Only

---

[3]   Still in Genesis 4:1.
[4]   See Genesis 3:16.

sacrifice. As you might expect, I have quite a lot to say about worship and sacrifice, but let's save Our longer chat about the subject for later. Suffice it for now to say that a sacrifice that functions in all the ways it's designed to work is one where the first and best of the harvest are given back to Me in an act that conveys, "This is yours. Actually, all of this is yours. It wouldn't be here if You didn't make it. I'm not making anything here – I'm just working with plants and animals that You already made by getting the line started and all. If it weren't for You, God, I'd have nothing; so thank you very much."

So the season ends, and Cain and Abel bring Me their sacrifices. Now, from all the movies you've seen, you may be thinking that the only kind of sacrifice around is an animal sacrifice, but in fact, anything can be sacrificed, or rather, offered as a sacrifice. It's basically anything that you offer to Me by permanently removing it from yourself. Back in the early days, this permanent removal was accomplished with fire, which consumes the grain, veggies or meat placed upon it. This brings along another nice anthropomorphized image of Me enjoying the smell of steak being offered up to Me as it sizzles over the crackling flames. I do love the smell of ribeyes in the morning. In Abel's case, it was lambchops. Also a very nice aroma.

The text points out that Abel – the shepherd – brings the fat of the first-born to me.[5] Long before people got idle enough to start worrying about their weight, fat was where it was at. Abel brings Me the best of the best available to him. The crème de la crème. That's the way, uh huh uh huh, I like it. A costly act of faith and beauty, like having a dozen long-stem roses waiting on the kitchen table for mom on her birthday. The text points out no such intentionality[6] on the part of Cain. Instead, like a lot of teenagers, he seems to slap something together without thinking much about it and that's what I get. A little like grabbing a 99-cent birthday card for mom from the bottom rack at the grocery store. Yes, there's some effort there, but hardly as much as is warranted.

Of course, I call him on it. And of course, I affirm Abel for his thoughtful and deliberate sacrifice of the best he has to offer. No such affirmation is forthcoming for the slapped-together sacrifice;[7] and like any sullen teenage sibling, Cain cops a major attitude when his kid brother gets the props instead of him. Cain is the firstborn here. He's the one who's supposed to be

---

[5] Genesis 4:4
[6] Compare Genesis 4:3 with 4:4. Keep noticing that sometimes there's just as much a lesson in what's not in the text as in what is in there.
[7] Genesis 4:4–5

setting the example, not Abel.[8] So Cain is suffering a couple layers of humiliation here. I've called him on his sketchy efforts, while at the same time his snot-nosed brother gets a blue ribbon.

But it's just one lousy mistake that Cain has made. You know what you do with mistakes? You learn from them, and do differently and better the next time. Which is exactly what I tell My still-buddy Cain, "Just do it right the next time, son, and everything'll be alright."[9] Not to keep banging the anvil about this point, folks, but make sure you recognize that at every junction, these young men are making choices. Abel chooses to sacrifice one way, Cain chooses to sacrifice another. Now Cain has to choose how to move on from what's happened – and this is huge, friends, so perk your ears – either learn from his mistake, or choose to usher sin into his heart and give it a front row seat.

Now, if it'd just have been Cain and Me, he'd have straightened up and flown right. But of course, it's not just Us. Little brother is in the mix, so enter the green monster.[10] Cain won't let go of the fact that he got a talking to when Able got an attaboy. And so, instead of Me, it is jealousy that gets the anachronistic driver's seat in Cain's heart, and it consumes him to the point that he kills his own brother. Now, I know those of you with brothers and/or sisters may have felt like killing them at times, but you didn't. Cain here is guilty of cold, pre-meditated murder: "Hey Abel, would you come check out the field with me this morning?" He's gone from haphazard teenager to murderer in just a couple sentences. How did Cain's transformation happen, and why does it matter?

Second question first. We're still firmly in prototype land here in the narrative, friend, and this story is just as much about sin and how it works (in you) as it is about Cain.[11] The stages Cain goes through are universal to the human experience, so keep an eye out for them.

So, how does his rapid downfall take place? He makes an initial mistake with his sacrifice – it's a little too careless and perfunctory. Hey, mistakes happen. Like I said, it's what Cain does with that mistake (and My acknowledgement of it) you have to watch out for. Instead of choosing to focus on himself (in a good way) and his relationship with Me, instead of

---

[8] And yes, the whole firstborn thing is going to be a running theme. Extra credit for noticing.
[9] Paraphrasing Genesis 4:5–7
[10] For you folks who live in Boston, I'm talking about jealousy, not your quirky ball field.
[11] And the ancestral line Cain establishes (as does his end-of-chapter-4 brother, Seth), is an aspect that is extremely important to the habitat that writes Genesis down.

taking advantage of the do-over I offer him (and you), he chooses instead to focus on Abel, and what Abel's got going on.

People, people, people. Take your eyes off other people, people. Put your eyes back on Me. Other people are not the source of life and goodness and beauty: I Am. Forget about the Joneses and the Smiths and the Bakers and the Candlestick Makers. You don't have to keep up with them, My friend. Keep up with yourself and where I'm leading you. Trust Me, you'll be far more fulfilled and at peace pursuing My life than you'd ever be pursuing theirs.

Cain's choice of focus – Abel instead of Me – is ultimately the undoing of them both as, in a way, both of them lose their lives. Abel's life is lost at the hands of his brother, but Cain's life is lost to what We're going to refer to as the downward spiral of sin. Cain had the chance to step back On The Way, but he didn't, so he moved deeper into sin. He's Our first clear example of the options before you, friend. You're always in motion: Either you're moving further On The Way, or deeper into the spiral. Instead of surrendering himself to Me, Cain surrenders to jealousy and slays his brother, and they both suffer permanent consequences. Abel breathes no more, and Cain is cast even further away from his folks and Me, and ends up settling in the land of Nod, east of Eden.[12]

So this quick story about two brothers (not the last pair of boys to whom We will point as an example) has a lot of meat to it, with strong lessons to mull over. Be intentional in your worship of Me. Accept My mercy and grace when I extend it to you (and I will), and take advantage of the do-over I offer you. Don't worry about what other people are doing or where they are in the grand scheme of things; worry about yourself, because living a life focused on and dictated by the lives of others is not going to end well.

While We've been looking at these two boys, I want you to notice a larger structure that has already kicked in. It's actually something that goes back to the starting edge. The opening chapters of Genesis depict a crescendo of sorts – the physical universe builds from day one in beauty and complexity, layer built upon layer, until this cosmic crescendo reaches its staggering climax: you. You can give that crescendo whatever name you want, just make it a positive one. The Love Crescendo. The God Crescendo. The God/Love Crescendo. The God Loves Me So Much He Saved the Best for Last Which Would Be Me Crescendo.

---

[12] Where James Dean will visit someday.

Another theme begins just about the time in Genesis 3 when Adam and Eve have a snack from the Choice Tree. It starts simply with one act of disobedience, but like the God/Love Crescendo, it builds layers and complexity as time goes on as you're starting to see. Mom and Dad kick the theme of sin off, then another layer is added by their sons, or rather, by Cain. Adam and Eve's sin ruptures the fabric of their relationship with one another, and their individual relationships with Me. Cain's sin extends the relational rupture to include siblings and brings about the very first death as a consequence. In this crescendo, the severity of sin and the severity of consequence are increasing. First, it is "only" relationship with Me that is impacted; then relationships between humans are compromised as well. The Human/Sin Crescendo moves on from there and builds, impacting not only individuals, but rippling out into communities. As more of the individuals who comprise those communities are caught up in the theme of self and sin, the layers of destruction build. Thus, as We move through Genesis, you'll find stories of catastrophic consequence from sin that climax in the stories of Noah,[13] and then of Babel.[14] Wiping out most humans with a do-over in the former only opens the way for a new crop of humans to do the same thing, so the second time the Human/Sin Crescendo reaches a climax at Babel, humanity is broken up into races and scattered across the earth in order to break or at least slow the crescendo cycle. Somewhat.

I don't want you to think We're going to spend forever in the first book of the Bible. For the love of Me, there are 38 more books to go![15] Don't worry, We're actually going to skip over a good bit of all the material there at your fingertips, though there are lessons to be learned from each book We've arranged to have in TOM. We'll course through other entries more quickly (mostly), but Genesis is different territory. Like We said, these stories are archetypes that lay the theological foundation for what follows. So let Me take a moment to make a couple of passing points about these two later archetypal stories of origin.

The tale of Noah and the ark is one of the most colorful out there in any kind of literature. It captures your imagination. It inspires nursery decorations, coloring books, plastic toys, and even stand-up comedy routines. Let's not deconstruct it all, but let's do notice a couple things. First, it underscores

---

[13] Genesis 6:9 – 9:29

[14] Genesis 11:1–9

[15] Even more in some of your more liturgical traditions. There are 39 books in total in the Tanakh and most First Testaments.

two of the main problems with sin: Given no barriers, sin is as pervasive and ever-increasing as crabgrass. Second, sin is serious business, and has to be dealt with. I simply can't throw up My hands and say, "Well, I guess kids will be kids." Letting you do as you will in order to learn from the consequences of your own mistakes only works if you reach that important point of actually learning. A final lesson from the whole humongous ark filled to the brim with animals is a reminder that this earth is not in fact all about just you. I made all of it. I love all of it. If I'm showing you how much I care for all creatures, it's a pretty good bet you need to follow My example. Now, there's all kinds of other nuance in Noah – go ahead and dig in on your own sometime – but the pervasive destructiveness of sin and the value of the rest of creation are primary takeaways.

The other big story that serves as the peak of the Humanity/Sin Crescendo Climax is the Tower of Babel. On the surface, this just looks like a myth thrown in to explain why there are different races on the earth. At first blush, these folks in Babel don't seem to be the reprobates that were Noah's pre-ark contemporaries, and in fact, they're not. Their sin is a horse of a different color, if you will. Instead of the great wickedness of Noah's neighbors, whose "every inclination of the thoughts of the human heart was only evil all the time,"[16] the evil that brings the crescendo to its climax at Babel is selfish, self-trusting ambition. The people don't seem to be carousing into the wee hours of the night; they're getting to bed early so they can be up at the crack of dawn in order to make a name for themselves. As it turns out, you still have people suffering from the same obsessive self-promotion who seek to make their name great just as their archetypes back in Babel do: They build a tower to the heavens and put their name on it. There's not a thought about Me or My provision of life or opportunity or – well, again, everything. It's all about them. They don't need to include, "This awesome tower is brought to you by my own awesomeness" underneath – that caption is assumed. "Look at how great we are! We're the kings of the world!" Really? Let's see about that.

What borders on hilarious in this quick, dense story[17] is that the people get themselves all worked up about this tower to the heavens that they're going to build with nothing but bricks and tar. That's the best they can do. And it's not going to last. It's not going to make it to the heavens to begin with, though they'll think and say it has. What bothers Me isn't their building

---

[16] Genesis 6:5 – image trying to sleep through those parties next door!
[17] That's Genesis 11:1–9 if you missed it the first time.

this tower so much as their mindset. It's like I don't even exist to these people, not even enough to give Me a, "We've got this one, God. You sit this one out." So their foolishness is underscored by the fact that these people are all that about some bricks and tar they'll slap together. Not exactly how I'd do it.

Now, if you're going ask Me to consult on or be part of a building project for an edifice that reaches to the heavens and lasts a very, very long time, I'm going give you better advice about your building materials. First point: Don't start with something *you*'ve made, as in bricks. Start with something that I've made, as in stone. Extrapolate that into looking at what exactly you're building your life out of right now. Is it human-made, or Me-made? Second, if you are going to erect a major structure in fact or metaphor, though you don't exactly need a divine building permit from Us, it is frankly unwise to enter into any significant endeavor without Our blessing. Unless you want the thing to fall on you.[18] But, of course, the story isn't about architecture, it's about attitude.

The flimsiness of their building materials, of course, underscores the temporary nature of whatever you're building on earth – whether it be a career, a reputation, or even an actual structure of stone and marble. You've got a handful of stone ruins peppered about the globe that testify to the fact that even the greatest human building projects surrender to time. In contrast, a life built with Me On The Way will not.

In Genesis 11, the people's pride and trust in themselves set them on a dangerous course seeking to place themselves essentially on Our level in order to gain the praise of others. Sounds a lot like what a lot of people are after these days in your habitat, friend, even if they're not operating at the scale of putting their names on buildings (well, at least *most* aren't). You don't need wealth to be self-absorbed, a rampant tendency in your time: eyes on themselves, trust in themselves, no need to look for or check in with Me. I Am not going to wipe these people on the plains of Shinar[19] from the earth, tempting as that may be. Neither am I going to wipe out New York, Los Angeles, Casper or Keokuk.[20] Besides, I've promised to level no more of that type of "do-over" in the wake of Noah's ark. However, I can't let humanity continue down this path to folly and destruction, thinking the whole time they're brilliant when all the while they're fools.

---

[18] Not that We're going to push it down on you; that'll happen all by itself.
[19] The tower town's named location before it gets its famous nickname because of the babble of new tongues born at its end (Genesis 11:2).
[20] This self-absorbed sin is by no means exclusive to major cities.

So I do humanity a huge archetypal favor and spread them out across the Earth into different races and languages[21] to help everyone remember how small they are; to help them remember their need for Me. Ultimately, it's to help them grow up, you could say, because, although the flavors of sin sported around Noah, Babel and Eden – or around Nashville, Baltimore, and East Seattle, for that matter – may manifest differently, they're still at their core an immature, ultimately damaging, centering on self. That's the core of sin – not taking others into consideration – not taking a lot of things into consideration, for that matter, Me especially.

The differences between the peoples have the same potential to (and will someday) be a source of awe and amazement, just as the other vast varieties in Our creation celebrate Our imaginative, beneficent power. However, that will come much, much farther down the road and On The Way. For now, the peoples of the earth are about as far from celebrating their differences as you are from the Andromeda galaxy.[22] The stain of selfishness and sin is still fresh and spreading quickly, and violence is on its way.

There's not much detail in the close of this final archetypal story, only the foundational formation of many languages scattered "abroad over the face of all the earth."[23] All that flows from this establishment of nations and cultures (and habitats) is easily inferred, though. For a good, long time, the eyes of the new nations necessarily continue to focus inward, but their gaze eventually lifts – in the very least in order to assess their neighbors' intentions. And assets. Most spring into conflict with each other, driven by the same green monster that felled Cain at the beginning of this chapter: competitive jealousy over resources, territory, wealth, water, whatever.

And so at the close of Genesis' opening chapters, the condition of humanity is a morass of sinful splintering selfishness, prideful competition, and violence inherent therein. This is the stage of the earth that is set for what We have planned to come next. The nature of The Owner's Manual will alter significantly after the Babel affair. While We will still be dealing with beginnings for a good while longer, We will shift modes from archetypal accounts to personal ones. We'll launch into those with the next chapter here, and let the genealogies that end Genesis 11 serve as a bridge between the two sections.

---

[21] Genesis 11:7–8

[22] That would be 2.5 million light years away. You can't get there from here, but We can.

[23] Genesis 11:9

Looking back, then, this opening section of Genesis which the tale of the tower is closing for Us serves as an introduction not only to that book but to the entire Manual. The outcome of Babel marks significant contrasts with how everything began. The consequences of humanity's sin have been laid bare on personal and planetary levels. The stark sketch of nations set to a certain course of conflict and conquest is intentionally antithetical to the peace, tranquility, and abundance of The Owner's Manual's opening paragraphs; those idyllic times of walking beside Me in the cool breezes of an afternoon, eating from trees laden with fine fruit; the sweetness of those simpler first days; the beauty of innocence and abundance side by side for all too short a time; all feeling quite distant by now.

Prideful, selfish sin separates humans from Us at that opening in Eden. Sin completes its ruinous course by separating humans from one another at the close in Babel. By the introduction's end, the toxic infection of sin is universal. However, deep within every human, no matter how sinful, lingers the foundational truth from Adam's first breath at the very beginning. However disguised you may become because of the paths you choose that lead away from Me, nothing you do or say can ever remove this element of your being on which all hope depends: I have made you in My image. You may have buried it deep within, but I Am here to tell you that We Are on a mission to restore all that has been lost. To awaken that noble image within you that slumbers beneath layers of hurt, brokenness and darkness. To speak life into you and call you Onto The Way that leads to everything We ever wanted for you, everything for which your true self longs. That journey will play out in a long single arc over the rest of TOM's pages, over the rest of time, in fact. And it all starts with one man who's willing to listen.

Chapter 7

The Gospel According to Abraham

Before the chapter holding the tale of Babel closes (that would be Genesis 11 if you're returning after a hiatus), you come across a seemingly annoying genealogy that draws a straight line from Noah (by his son, Shem) to Our next primary character, Abram.[1] Before We take a look at The A Man, let Me help you be a little less annoyed by the genealogies in The Owner's Manual. Like every other part of the Bible, they're there for a reason: their purpose.[2] This actually links quite a bit with some of the lessons about to spring from Abram. For one thing, those long lists of so-and-so fathering so–and–so underscore that everyone who plays a part in this drama is a plain old regular person. They're members of families – somebody's son who grows up to be someone else's dad. These are not people descended from Mount Olympus with special abilities. As if. They're regular folks just like you and your family; and since they're like your family, clearly, none of them are perfect.

Another idea carried by these long lists of mostly fathers and sons[3] is that of legacy. Just like you and/or your parents – at least when they're thinking about it and not just going through the day on autopilot – these ordinary people are taking very seriously what they are passing on to the next generation in terms of their identity, their understanding of the world, and their understanding of Me in particular. Yes, it's a habitat function on one

---

[1] Genesis 11:10–26.

[2] Just had to use all three.

[3] There are a few exceptions to this with the occasional listing of a woman in these genealogies, but the era we're about to enter is the definitive Patriarchal Age. (You can thank Me you weren't born into that habitat, dear daughters.) As such, when a woman gets in one of these lists, she's exceedingly exceptional.

level, but it's far more than that because I Am in the picture, and I transcend culture. So one of the points of listing the line from Noah to Abram is to notice the legacy of faithfulness that travels down the generations of ordinary people from Noah – who was chosen for his mission because he was a righteous man who walked with Me[4] – generation after generation until his great[5] grandson is chosen for his own mission, should he choose to accept it.

Now, it's perfectly fine that a whole lot of studious readers draw a line at the end of Genesis 11 because the nature of what's going on shifts away from those earlier archetypal events which function as broader explanations of how things are: the natural world, sin and evil, temptation, rainbows, languages, nations, all kinds of fun stuff. After the tales of Adam, Cain, Noah and Babel finish, the camera focuses in far more closely and the action assumes a much slower pace as We walk quite awhile with Abram. The scholars say We shift from protohistory to patriarchs from chapter 11 to chapter 12, respectively. Though We've already acknowledged a noticeable change in the narrative at this point, I Am not going to draw a formal dividing line here. Regardless of the human need to categorize things, let Us point out that the seed that bears Abram is tucked right there into Noah (physically *and* spiritually); so, as far as We're concerned, the story is just continuing when We get to chapter 12. But if you insist on slicing the book into two parts, then by all means notice that The Plan has begun and is underway before the curtain closes on your protohistorical introduction. The Plan is there from (and before) the very beginning. It's not a "woops," a do-over, or Plan B. It's Plan A with The A man, Our man Abram. He's a prototype all by himself anyway.

Now, you may be wondering what's wrong with the print you're reading – I've been saying "Abram" instead of "Abraham." As in "Father Abraham" – the one who apparently had the many sons some of you sang about when you were kids while adding all your limbs in succession to a hokey-pokesque choreography designed to erase all meaning whatsoever from the story.[6] If you were spared this particular exercise in your childhood yet are still a bit puzzled, let Us make it easier on everyone: Abram and Abraham are the

---

[4] Genesis 6:8–9.
[5] This looks like a footnote but is actually the mathematical magnitude code meaning "to the fifth power."
[6] I obviously understand and do like the point of the song, but Abra(ha)m had two sons in his "early" life, then six more with another wife after his first wife's passing (Gen 25:1). We'll look at the first set.

same fellow. His father, Terah, gave him the name of Abram,[7] which means "the Father (referring to Me) is exalted." You can see why I took a liking to The A Man from his very beginning. His name is going to stay Abram for quite a while, and I'm the One who's going to change it eventually, but We'll get to that. You don't get to know much at all about Abram's dad, Terah. His being Abram's dad is pretty much his big claim to fame. Not that I don't want you to shoot for anything impressive or substantial with your life, but if you're a parent, keep in mind that the greatest thing you may be doing with your life is raising the next Abram. Yep. Time to start getting home from work before the kids are asleep. Your legacy lies with them, friend. Not your career. Really.

Okay, off the soap box for a while. Let's look at Abram. This guy has a bland, normal life until the ripe age of 75. Normal with the exception of *not* having any kids. And it was different in Abram's habitat than it is in yours now – then, no one was *ever* choosing to not have kids because of their desire for an ambitious career or their dislike of random elements in their lives. Carrying on the family line had immense weight for this habitat.

Remember, this is very early in Our relationship with humanity, and very early in humans' theological development, so the concept of an eternity of time in a life after physical death isn't something they can process yet on at least two levels. First, large numbers – or the conception of them – don't even exist at this point, much less the notion of an uncountable "eternity." Add to that the habitatual skew inherent in your time: Most of you grew up being taught that your life is going to continue eternally after your body dies. (Yes, I know what I said before about Plato, and don't worry, We'll work it all out before We're done.) Life after death is actually woven into your habitat's thinking now, with obvious exceptions. No such thinking was possible for Abram or anyone else for a good thousand years or so after him. My point? The only way for someone to have a sense of their life continuing in any fashion after death in Abram's time is for their life to live on in their children. Thus, everybody in his habitat wants kids, but Abram has none at 75, and since his beautiful wife Sarai is only 10 years his junior and has yet to bear any children, that chapter is firmly closed for them at this point. They are no longer a natural resource when it comes to offspring.

---

[7] Actually, Terah gave him the name Avram, which was pronounced Av-RAHM, with the stress on the second syllable. The Hebrew consonant for your letter "v" doubles as a "b" at times, which has led to generations of gentile/goyim mispronunciation. Most people think it's not that big a deal, but I personally prefer being called "God" much more than "Got." We'll stick with "Abram," though, for clarity's sake.

So check out the first four verses of Genesis 12, keeping in mind I'm talking to a 75-year-old man with a post-menopausal, barren, 65-year-old wife. Once again, I'll wait for you. Go on, now. These are some of the most important sentences in TOM, so I don't want to enable your blowing off the reading by summarizing them. Get out My Book. Please.[8]

Everyone in Abram's habitat lives in multi-generational households. At the point of life in which we find Abram in 12:1, sticking with his extended family and being a positive influence on his nieces and nephews is the closest thing to legacy Abram and Sarai are going to achieve. The text just before[9] casually mentions that Abram's brother, Haran, has three children: two daughters and a son. Haran dies at a young age, so his (and Abram's) brother Nahor marries one of Haran's girls so she's looked after (yes, another habitat norm), and Abram seems to take Haran's boy, Lot, under his wing and treats him like a son.

All that is to say that the family Abram comes from is a normal family of its time, relying on one another, three or four generations all together. So for Me to ask Abram to leave behind his family and the land in which they live in order to strike out into unknown territory with Me – when he'll be separating himself from the only support network available to him – is asking a whole heck of a lot. Especially in view of his and Sarai's advancing age.[10] Note that I don't even tell him where We're going to end up with him. Think about that tidbit a moment. I just tell him to leave *everything* behind – his country, people, and family – and strike out *into the unknown* with Me. "Head that-a-way" is all Abram gets from Me.

Alright. It's driving Me nuts. I know some of you haven't looked it up. So, here. Just this once:

> Now the LORD said to Abram, "Go from your country and your kindred and your father's house to the land that I will show you. I will make of you a great nation, and I will bless you, and make your name great, so that you will be a blessing. I will bless those who bless you, and the one who curses you I will curse; and in you all the families of the earth shall be blessed."

---

[8] Don't forget online options. If you still haven't done so, a quick search for "bible online" will set you up. Add a level of commitment by installing an app!

[9] Genesis 11:27–29.

[10] Those may be fine early years of retirement in Florida with the family and its demands left behind up north, but then when your body starts falling apart and the support network of the following generation(s) is a thousand miles away, you may wish you'd never left home.

So Abram went, as the LORD had told him; and Lot went with him. Abram was seventy-five years old when he departed from Haran.[11]

Now, the whole point of reading all this – in both TOM and this volume – is not just to learn a few bits of interesting information, but to interact with Us in a way that refreshes your walk through life. So We must pause again at this point to point out that there will be times when you've got some parallels to Abram's story in yours. As long as We're pointing, the case in point is Abram's call. There's a whole lot We Are going to help you learn from it, and the first tidbit is what We just mentioned. His call is limited at first. We don't reveal to him the whole breadth of Our plan for him. In fact, We only tell him what he needs to know to get started: leave. Inherent in this is an expectation on Our part (and a trust on his) that more information will be provided On The Way once Abram obeys the first call.

I Am going to work with you the same way, friend. You may be in a situation that is harmful to you, though not necessarily so – you may simply be shackled to the mundane and ordinary – and I have something far greater in mind for you. Just as I work with Abram on levels at which he can relate, I'll call you first away from the situation you're in, often without a clear picture of where We're going. Sometimes it's necessary to step away from all that you comfortably trust and rely on in order to stretch your imagination and faith, to build your belief muscle to a greater strength so it can handle a bigger load later on down the road. Of course, I'm not saying to throw caution to the winds and pack your bags and leave tonight. Not necessarily, that is; however, don't be surprised if that feeling of unsettledness doesn't always come with a full exposition of your final destiny at the moment. You'll know if I'm nudging you to step away and out in faith. If you're up to no good (and you know it),[12] then there's no question that the right thing to do is leave that party immediately. You also know, however, whether you're in a place where you will not reach your potential with Us because the environment in which you live expects so little of you. By stepping out and away, you and Abram open yourselves up to all kinds of new options and paths that simply were not possible from the static starting point of the past.

---

[11] Genesis 12:1–4, NRSV.
[12] We Are not saying that Abram's behavior is bad at this point, just using him as an example of leaving the past behind.

If Abram remains in the situation of life as it always has been, there may be the comfort of sameness to look forward to every morning, but there will not be hope. No future generation will rise from him; his name and story will end with his last breath. No, the only hope Abram has is to leave the known and step out On The Way to which We Are calling him. To step out of the past into the future. Every future is by definition unknown, whether you have a guess of what it will look like or not. Abram doesn't have even a sketch of it, but he knows enough – he hears enough – to know that it starts with stepping away from the old, hopeless life into the new one We Are calling him toward. Like Abram, you have the choice of hearing Our call to a greater life in Us, or of staying in your version of Ur and maintaining the status quo and worshiping the local gods of comfort and ease. That's a sentence that bears rereading.

Abram is leaving those gods of comfort and ease behind along with other local deities. Though it's not explicit in the text,[13] one can also infer that I Am also asking him to leave behind the gods of his old neighborhood: the city of Ur[14] of the Chaldeans, who had a thing for a moon god by the name of Nanna. Nanna's not your grandmother this time. He's actually a male god overseeing cycles of fertility, whether they be the monthly turn of female mammals or the turn of season from winter to spring or dry to rainy. That Abram and Sarai have to leave Nanna's territory to eventually find fertility is an ironic testimony to the moon god's impotence.

The fact that neither Nanna nor his deific neighbors get a mention in My Book is another clue about how I'm dealing with you all as a race across the millennia. Not wanting to acknowledge the other "gods" in any way, I Am very rarely going to mention any of them by name. To do so would make it seem like I conceded their existence (which I do not). This runs deeper than the logic behind "I'm not going to dignify that with a response," and includes Our maintaining as distraction-free a course both for Abram and for those reading his account in TOM across the ages. There really is no need to research ancient Mesopotamian "deities" to know how to step out in faith and follow My call as Abram does. Sure, go ahead and see what's back there if you like, but don't get too distracted. I Am the One you should be investigating, not the non-existent no-shows across the habitats and ages.

---

[13] Until Joshua 24:1–2, that is.
[14] Genesis 11:28, 31; 15:7.

And speaking of time, how I'm working with Abram in stages – not overwhelming him with too much at once, revealing more as We go along – is another universal pattern for My work with you humans. I'm taking My time with you because I know that's going to work best. As I said, I'm meeting you where you are and carrying you further On The Way as We go along together. There are some things in Abram's life that I'm eventually going to work toward easing out not during his lifetime but over millennia as habitats come and go: slavery, the denigrated social status of women, and ubiquitous polytheism, to name but a few. As far as the last one goes, at this point, I'm not even on a campaign to make Abram think I'm the only god on the block, just that I'm the One who's got his back.

In fact, he thinks I'm just one of the gods on the menu at the time – the high god *El* of the Canaanites, who not by coincidence was believed to have made the universe (but who also was believed to have been the father of Baal, a "god" whose name appears later in the story [he, of course, never does]). However, as I prove Myself faithful across the ages and the other gods prove themselves fruitless and fictional (especially when we hit Egypt here in a little while), it'll begin to dawn on folks that all those other deities were things people came up with on their own as a way to explain the conviction they felt that there was something greater than them out there reigning over it all, holding the reins, in and out of the rain! Practically every indigenous culture on every scrap of the planet felt a yearning for something greater – that heart/soul hole only We can fill – and came up with something based on what they could see and know on their own to explain the greatness outside themselves. We can and have used that across the ages.

However, what I'm doing with Abram is something new, different, and designed for the long haul. I Am starting the process of revealing Myself directly to humanity, and I'll be working on refining and fine-tuning humanity's understanding of Me for the rest of time. There are major highlights of this process in TOM, and We're going to look at a good number of them. I want you to note here at the start of Our journey with Abram, though, that We Are still helping you understand Us more – you as the human race, and you as you the person reading right now. You're all a work in progress, and We're not going to quit on you until We see you face to face again. Let's not get ahead of Ourselves, though. For now, I'm meeting you and Abram right where you both live in a unique way suited to your perception and situation.

So I'm asking Abram to leave Nanna behind and come to Poppa, to put all his eggs (and Sarai's) in one basket: Me. Then I begin what I like to call

The Plan. It's The Plan that will consume the rest of Our time together with you. The Plan that undoes the damage done at The Choice Tree, redeems the hurt and injury done by all other sin in history, restores humanity's relationship with Us, renders death itself powerless in the end, and makes the final phase possible – that face to face bit I just mentioned. It's the great, big, fat, hairy deal and the primary point of The Owner's Manual: The Plan. And it all begins with Abram right here in Genesis 12. The rest of the entire Manual, the rest of history itself, is going to be the working out of Our promises to Abram. So pay attention.

The rescue of all humanity doesn't start with an army, or a king, or a prophet, or anyone particularly remarkable at all. It starts with this guy as normal as your neighbor (the normal neighbor, not the crazy one). Actually it starts with an old guy and his wife who in and of themselves don't have what it takes to do anything. What Abram does have – the only thing he brings to the table, in fact – is the ability to believe that *I* will do what *I* say *I* will do. He's not going to do it. I Am. But to do so I need a human partner, and because Abram's got just enough faith and taste for adventure, together We put in motion The Plan that ends with you reading this right now about Us.[15] And so, to honor this simple man who is the start of it all, We'll be calling Our Plan for humanity's rescue the "Abraplan" from now on. Feel free to use the term in discussion or doctoral theses if you like.

We are stressing Abram's normality for obvious reasons. You, also, are pretty normal. Yes, We know about your unique quirks, but all in all, from where We stand, you're not much different from Abram. And if you don't think you have what he's got, then keep reading. We cannot stress enough this simple fact: Abram is an ordinary guy who supplies the only thing he can bring to the equation. He believes. Yes, he's got a body, and so does Sarai, but those are barely useful; useful only, in fact, if I get involved. No, Abram's important possession is belief. Belief is only as strong as the object it believes in, and fortunately for Abram, I Am the object of his belief.

Abram believes Me when I tell him that I'm going to make him into "a great nation" – as in: His offspring and the generations to follow are going to burst into such huge numbers they're going to be their own country. Abram believes Me when I tell him I'm going to slather so many blessings on him

---

[15] Of course, that's not where it all ends, but We're going to stay linear with you since that's how you process things.

that *all* families[16] on earth will be blessed through his family. His family that doesn't exist (yet), that doesn't seem feasible – an impossible key unlocking the future and impacting every family on earth, all the way down through time to yours.

Given the fact that so much is promised, Abram and Sarai are the perfect couple with which to start The Plan, because their infertility, and more precisely, Sarai's infertile womb, is the most unlikely place possible for a sprawling nation to have its conception. The only way this is going to happen is if I get involved. Which I have every intention of doing, seeing as I promised the barren couple they'd have at least one child (notice I didn't promise them a slew of kids themselves, just that their line would continue and thrive, thus, a single son[17] can satisfy the promise). To make it even more clear that I Am the one who's going to bring about the promised offspring, I've separated Abram from his extended family so there'll be no borrowing members of the next generation from amongst his nieces and nephews to construct and try to make it happen on their own. (If you're thinking about Lot [Abram's storied nephew], as We mentioned earlier, even though Abram is looking out for the guy, if you know the big points in his story, it's quite clear Lot is not Abram's son.)

As I mentioned, here at the opening of Genesis 12 are some of the most important sentences ever written. The importance of My promise to Abram cannot be underestimated. It's still in force today, still working its way out, so important you may tire of My talking about it. However, none of those opening verses has more power per syllable than the first three words of verse 4: "So Abram went." Say it out loud to yourself. So Abram went. If he hadn't, you wouldn't be reading this.

With nothing to go on but My promise, he leaves everything he knows – and everything his habitat tells him is important – and steps out into the unknown, believing I will come through for him and keep My (still rather indistinct) promises. Since he is step one in The Plan – and puts the "Abra" in "Abraplan" – it's not like he's got anything to look back on. For the rest of The Owner's Manual, people are going to be able to look back on the record of My faithfulness to others (starting with Abram) and take courage from it; however, Abram has *nothing* to look back on but perhaps some broad

---

[16] Your translation may read "all peoples on earth," which is a natural inference from the "all families" that are literally there in Hebrew. I do prefer the family reference to its extrapolation. "All families" keeps the whole plan operating at the household level.

[17] Another habitat requirement.

stroke, large scale tales that focus on why things are rather than on anything remotely close to a working partnership with Me. All he's got to go on right now is a handful of My words[18] to him. Still, he believes Me and goes. "So Abram went," with the destiny of all families on earth for the rest of time hanging in the balance. Sure enough. Good man.

This is the primary lesson from Abram, and one that will be repeated over and over in both the positive and negative sense in Our journey with humanity: Abram believes Me, and so he takes action. Faith in what I Am saying – faith that I will keep the promises I Am making – yields obedience to My instruction. Abram believes Me, so he obeys Me. You see, believing something isn't simply agreeing to it on an intellectual level. It is taking in that knowledge fully, internalizing it into your frame of reference, and then (main point) basing your actions upon it. Believing Us and Our message is going to change the way you live. It's going to move out from your brain where you understand it into your body where you'll live it. Thinking something is true is one thing. Living like it's true is another. Abram believes Me, and as a result, he takes that first step away from the life he's known and walked for seventy something years into unknown territory with nothing to go on but My whisper in his ear. See Abram go. Go, Abram, go.

And so, Abram's and Sarai's families are in the rear-view mirror, along with their youth and any chance of natural fertility. One of the ways in which We do Our best work with humans is in situations like this: I've promised something impossible, and the only hope of its taking place is that I be the one to make it happen – not humanity or the course of "nature." Nature has run its course for these two older folks and left them childless; however, I Am (quite obviously) above nature, super-natural.

So Abram's already a multi-faceted template for Our interaction with humanity. We've called him away from his old life toward a new one We've promised but not yet defined; he's believed Us enough to step out in faith towards that new life; and the promises We've made to Abram can't happen without Our intervention. There'll be no pulling himself up by his sandalstraps and making things happen. It really is all on Us to override nature if the Abraplan is going to move forward.

---

[18] To be precise, 27 words in Hebrew. They've got a far more efficient pronoun system that attaches to their verbs and nouns, so it takes 72 words in English to translate; you're not getting any extra material, though.

However, We don't exactly make Abram's head spin with how quickly it all comes to pass. You see, another feature of Our work together with humans is that they are always in a much bigger rush than We Are. This is actually mostly a function of the previous feature – the longer We wait, the clearer it is that it's Us making it happen, not humans, and not "luck." But once again, there's more to it than that. The waiting process is the only class-room where trust and faith are able to really grow.

This is particularly true for Abram, who as We said, doesn't have a vol-ume of precedents to look back on to see My record. Therefore, his trust in Me is going to come about the old-fashioned way: He's going to have to experience My promise-keeping himself on smaller levels so that He'll know He can trust My bigger as-yet-to-be-fulfilled promises too. And for some of you, even though you do have a volume of precedents, you don't trust it very much and so require your own subjective experiences before you'll trust Me fully. Fine. I can work with that. Obviously, you've got a bit of Abram in you already, or you wouldn't be reading this.

By now you've noticed that there's a great deal packed into this handful of verses, and though there's even more to say about them, let's let Abram go ahead and get some miles under his belt. He's grown up beside the Euphrates River in Ur, in southeast Mesopotamia just northwest of the Persian Gulf.[19] Now he pulls up stakes and moves clear to the other (northwest) corner of Mesopotamia, a good 600 miles, to the crossroads town of Harran.[20] Along with him travels his father, Terah, while the old man is still alive.[21] So when you get to the critical phrase "So Abram went" in 12:4, Abram is at that point going from Harran, not Ur, which is a good thing. This way he's only got roughly 400 miles to cover before We tell him to stop, rather than the full 1,000 from back in Ur.

When We call him to leave, Abram leaves Harran, still his homeland if not his hometown. Sort of like calling you to live overseas after you've moved from Georgia to Idaho (or to emigrate to the U.S. after you've moved from Hastings to Liverpool, or…). They set off to the south and west, crossing the border into Canaan, traveling farther into it until they arrive at its heart in the town of Shechem,[22] nestled in the hills between the Mediterranean

---

[19] Southeastern Iraq in your habitat.
[20] Southern Turkey along its border with Syria in your habitat.
[21] Genesis 11:31–32.
[22] Genesis 12:6–7.

Sea and the Jordan River. There is a great terebinth tree[23] there, respected as sacred and known as a place to receive inspired teaching, and indeed I appear to Abram there and say, "This is it, Abram. To your seed I will give this land."[24]

Finally, a little more information. Now Abram knows where he's going, but – don't miss this part – he doesn't realize what his destination is *until he gets there*. I take full responsibility for this. This process has been an important one in building Abram's faith. Every day on his journey of hundreds of miles, he's awakened wondering if that's the day. He's had to live in a place of trust, of journey between the points of the past and the promise. I know you can identify with the tension latent in this dynamic as well. This is not something I do arbitrarily, but rather something that brings the best out of you in time. If We had told Abram We were calling him on a 400 mile hike to find a better life – much less a 1,000 mile one – he'd have told Me, "Take a hike yourself, thank you very much. Things are just fine here." If We were to tell you where We Are ultimately going to bring you, you'd also be overwhelmed and balk at beginning.

Just for fun, do two minutes of research to find someplace about 400 miles from where you live so you can put yourself in Abram's sandals. New Yorkers would be walking to Niagara Falls, San Franciscans to Los Angeles, Londoners to Glasgow, Melbourners to Canberra, etc., and vice versa. Abram walked that distance one day at a time, each day starting with a small but important first step, not knowing where those steps would lead. Now turn that parable on your own life. Look how far you've come from where you used to be, especially if you're already On The Way. All that good was done one day at a time. Today's the only day you can do anything with, so you may as well do the most you can with it, even if it's just taking some simple steps in the right direction à la Abram. Do the same tomorrow, and there's no telling how far you'll get with Me On The Way.

Having arrived at the land We'd been promising, Abram has the reward of a fulfillment of trust in Me, trust he's exhibited while waiting for more information. Trust revealed in each day spent walking further into the unknown in obedience to Our admittedly very incomplete call. Take note of

---

[23] Long limbs and unique leaves create a cave-like cool beneath these giants.

[24] Most translations soften the biological term "seed" to "offspring," but the word I use is the same as later in Deuteronomy 28:38, referring to seed that's going to get planted in the ground. Note My poetic placement of such a pledge: Abram's small, withered seed is promised to make a nation, just as a wee dry seed has made the great terebinth under which he rests.

that dichotomy, friend. Waiting on Me involves action, not lethargy. Moving forward, not sitting still. Abram is waiting for Me to fulfill and flesh out My promise to him, but he is doing so while actively obeying what little he does know already. He only arrives at the point of further disclosure because he has been faithful to his introductory call; now Abram's faith is made that much stronger by the exchange of hope for the realization of arrival.

This arrival is a hugely important step, but it's only the beginning. We'll continue to reveal more to Abram and every other human as their journey continues; all in steps that require, build, and then affirm faith in a continual process. We reveal to Abram the fact that he's arrived in the land of promise after he's finished the long hike; however, the voyage is far from over.

Although it's clear that Abram enters the drama with a good bit of faith – enough to do as I say in 12:4 with little evidence he should do so – he's going to need even more before he's through. We therefore have to take Our time with him to give his belief muscles time to grow. The baby I've promised him and Sarai doesn't exactly come right along as soon as they reach the land of Canaan. Oh, Abram thinks so, or at least acts like it. First, on receiving the good news that he's walking on the land I'm giving his seed/offspring, he builds an altar to Me right there at the sacred tree and sends up thankful worship. (You don't need a full paragraph pointing out what a good example that is for you at major moments in your life, do you?) He then moves to open land southeast of town and pitches his small household's tents beside a cozy river there. Abram builds another altar here as if planning to stay a while, for it seems that he and Sarai are home, and their new beginning is under way. There should be some morning sickness right around the corner, right?

However, I didn't actually say it was time to settle in this land, just that this is the land in which the descendents of your seed are going to dwell. Yes, that's a bit of a technicality, but Abram's already picking up on the fact that what I do not say is often as important as what I do. Without a clear word from Me to remain there beside the river, he moves gradually southward in the open country, expecting another word at any moment to tell him it is finally time to settle.

Take another personal note here, then, in the way Abram's journey is playing out in parallel to yours. Often, the place you're striving toward as what you think to be your final destination is merely a resting point: a necessary goal On The Way at which to pause for a time until the next goal arises which will move you further toward that actual destination which all the other goals are serving. If you're on the jaded side, you may think of this as a bait-and-switch technique on My part; I prefer the term "incremental revelation."

Speaking of increments, Abram's only completed the first leg of his expedition, and his belief muscles are going to have to be much stronger for what's in store, stronger than they're going to get from a simple 400 mile road trip. In fact, years go by with one diversion after another in which Abram's going to have to pretty much hang in there, just like he did when traveling from home to Canaan, not knowing when he was going to arrive.

His first detour appears not long after the old couple arrives in Canaan when a famine hits the land, and the only place any food can be found is down in Egypt, a place of far-reaching power. Abram has known men of power in Ur. He knows how they think and act. I mentioned earlier Sarai's great beauty: Despite her age, men still stop whatever they're doing when she walks by so they can gaze at her. Abram rightly fears that some powerful Egyptian will want her beauty and kill him to get her since he's her husband.

It's important to note that I do not tell Abram to go to Egypt. No, I've said I would bless and care for him. Abram's the one who decides to go to Egypt, not necessarily in disobedience, but... definitely trusting more in what makes sense to him at the time rather than in My promises of blessing.

Think about this dynamic in your life, friend, and I know you'll easily come up with some moments like this. Times when you wake up and find yourself operating on your own, relying solely on yourself. Most times, these self-trust moments don't end well, and you can bet We'll see plenty such examples in TOM as We go along.

So from fear of starving, it makes sense to Abram to take Sarai to Egypt. Then from fear of getting murdered, it also makes sense to him that his identity as husband of Sarai be concealed, and so he instructs her to tell anyone who asks that she's his sister.[25] As expected, when they arrive in Egypt, word spreads quickly that a stunningly beautiful woman is among the incoming refugees. Reports spread all the way to Pharaoh, and he takes her into his palace. Thinking Abram her brother because of the promulgated deception, Pharaoh gives him piles of wealth in gratitude: sheep, cattle, donkeys, slaves, camels. Though he is of some means before this, Abram is instantly prosperous.

---

[25] Actually half true on their father's side (Genesis 20:12) but still used solely to deceive.

I Am not pleased, however. Pharaoh's entire household is struck with illness;[26] it is made known to Pharaoh that this has come upon him in punishment for taking Abram's wife as his. The king returns Sarai to Abram, justifiably angry at their subterfuge, then sends Abram, Sarai, and their entire growing entourage away with orders that none of them be touched, down to the last sheep, lest Abram's God plague Pharaoh further.

Now, you're right to take issue with how things turn out here. It's patently unfair that Pharaoh be punished for something he doesn't know. Here is perhaps the first example of consequence falling on the innocent. Because of Abram's and Sarai's lie about her identity, Pharaoh unwittingly takes a married woman to be his wife. While justice would dictate that Abram suffer the consequence,[27] his is minor compared to others'.

You see, by trusting in his own instincts instead of My promises, Abram has jeopardized the entire Plan with his self-protecting lie. How are all the families of the earth supposed to be blessed through his seed if his wife is now married to Pharaoh? If the consequence falls on Abram right now, the Abraplan is finished before it's begun. However, a consequence-free status quo is just as final, for it leaves Sarai married to Pharaoh. The only thing We can do at this point is something that will move Pharaoh to reject her and send her back to Moses. Non-fatal yet annoying illness all around the palace does the trick, and Sarai is soon returned to her proper place with Abram.

The lesson from this episode isn't that you can get away with lying, though frankly, Abram does seem to here. Rather, it's that your self-trust isn't just going to come back and bite you in the consequences; it's going to impact the people around you. Abram may be leaving Egypt with an abundance of livestock now, but he'll be known forever as a liar. Yes, We will point to his faith as an example, but as his story is told in all future generations, there'll be a moment where it must be said, "but he lied about his wife..."

Obviously Sarai and Pharaoh's entire household feel the fallout from Abram's lie as well. The text never says that Sarai ever lay in consummation with Pharaoh – or that she refused him – but Pharaoh calls her his wife[28] and married her not for political reasons but for her beauty. In the very least she is made to endure many uncomfortable situations, and very likely a sense of personal shame and disgrace until the warning shots of illness hit the royal

---

[26] "Serious diseases" in the NIV (Genesis 12:17 – 12:10–20 for the whole episode).
[27] Sarai's guilt is far lesser in all of this, as she's simply been obeying Abram all along.
[28] Genesis 12:19.

family. Yes, the ripples from Abram's sin reach out into the lives of many near and far from him and do deep harm. Keep that in mind the next time you're tempted to follow Abram's poor instant example and trust in your own wiles rather than in Me. Learn from him to keep an eye out for trusting too much in your strength and understanding. If anything, this entire sequence in Egypt testifies to a lapse and lack of it.

No longer welcome in Egypt but now amply supplied by her to withstand what remains of the famine, Abram's growing entourage guides his expanded flocks and herds back to Canaan. (Abram gives half of Pharaoh's gifts to Lot as his own.) They move back through the Negev, eventually to return to the spot beside the river outside Shechem where they'd first pitched their tents.[29]

Now, though, there is simply too much livestock between Lot and Abram to be sustained there; the area would be overgrazed in no time. Before long, their herdsmen are fighting with one another over who gets to pasture where. And so Abram decides it is time to send his nephew, whom he'd treated like a son, off on his own, giving him his choice of all the land before them. Some would say Lot dishonors his old uncle by choosing what seems to be the best – the plains beside the Jordan – but Abram genuinely wants him to succeed, and is honest in the offer.[30]

And here's the reason you get all the herding, overgrazing detail. It is just after Lot leaves that I come to Abram again and tell him to stand up and say:

> "Raise your eyes now, and look from the place where you are, northward and southward and eastward and westward, for all the land that you see I will give to you and to your offspring forever. I will make your offspring like the dust of the earth, so that if one can count the dust of the earth, your offspring also can be counted. Rise up, walk through the length and the breadth of the land, for I will give it to you."[31]

Every time I speak to Abram, My promises increase: the dimensions of the land I Am promising, and the amount of Abram's offspring. First it was just a patch of land in the hills, now it's everywhere he can see. First it was

---

[29] Genesis 13:1–4.
[30] Genesis 13:5–7.
[31] Genesis 13:14–17, NRSV.

just "a great nation," now the descendants from Abram's seed are as count-less as the specks of dust of the earth. Rewarding his faith, I reveal more as the journey continues and Abram's trust in Me grows. I have promised to bless him, and surely have, so much so that he and Lot have to split up over their bounteous livestock. Abram has a growing sense that I Am with him, that I Am protecting and caring for him, and so We can let him in on more of The Plan, still working with him where he's at in terms of perception, understanding, and faith.

A further important example of this comes a few years later. At My urg-ing to "walk through the length and the breadth of the land,"[32] Abram does so, requiring more than an afternoon stroll. He has to pull up his tent stakes and trek over it all with his entire household, eventually settling some 50 miles further south from where We'd first said in Shechem, "Here's the land!" Abram establishes himself down in Mamre in a valley cooled by great tere-binth trees not unlike that sacred tree up in Shechem. He builds a third altar to Me there, worshipping and thanking Me for blessing him richly, which I continue to do as the time passes. Abram's flocks and herds grow, along with his alliances with his neighbors.

Lot, however, is not so blessed. He is captured in a skirmish between warring city kings in the region in which he has chosen to live.[33] Because Lot is like a son to Abram, the old man launches out with all the slaves in his household[34] that are trained for battle, along with all the allies Abram's made among the local Amorites, and they pursue Lot's captors. With a surprise attack from different sides during the night, they recover not only Lot and all his possessions, but all the other captured goods and people as well.

What happens on their way back is why We're giving you all these details. As Abram's band escorts all the freed captives back to their towns, their kings come out to meet them all with great joy. One of the kings, Melchizedek, the king of Salem, is a priest of *EL ELYON*, "God Most High" – the name of the chief Canaanite god, whom We've mentioned. Melchizedek brings out bread and wine before Abram, blessing him and saying, "Blessed be Abram by *EL ELYON*, Creator of heaven and earth, and praise be to *EL ELYON*, who has delivered your enemies into your hand."[35]

---

[32] Genesis 13:17–18.
[33] Genesis 14.
[34] Skilled "gifts" from Pharaoh.
[35] Genesis 14:17–20.

Now, do I step in and clarify things at this point? "Excuse Me, but let Me straighten out this confusion, folks..." Nope. I Am working even through this Canaanite priest, who recognizes that there is a Most High God Who's made everything. He's just a bit misinformed about My address. Yes, I'm in Canaan, but not just there. We Are in this for the long haul, and there will be other times and encounters in which to expand Abram's (and his seed's) understanding of Us. For now, Melchizedek and Abram are both sincerely giving Us credit in the way they know for the successful rescue of the prisoners.

There's another deed to notice in this, tucked away as the last sentence in the Scripture that two of you just read as you looked up the last footnote cited in TOM. In this very first encounter Abram has with someone he considers to be one of My priests, Abram gives Melchizedek one tenth of everything that's just been gained in that overnight attack. Reasoning that it is his solely through Our blessings, as Melchizedek has just said, Abram offers a full tenth – also known as a tithe – in praise and thanksgiving. Sure, there've been plenty of sacrifices made to Me in TOM already, starting way back with Cain and Abel, but this is the first formal tithe, something to remember as a precedent set here with The A Man. Tuck that into your awareness for now, and We'll examine it later.

One final major moment is associated with this whole rescue of Lot. Once the nephew is seen safely home, Abram and his men make their way to theirs. Asleep again in his own tents, and right on the heels of his encounter with the priest, I come to Abram again: "Do not be afraid, Abram. I Am your shield, your very great reward."[36]

His reply is understandable. Abram calls Me on not giving him an heir yet, though sufficient, significant time has passed since My promise. He notes that, if he were to drop dead at this moment, one of his slaves would inherit his estate (which I've kept building for him, keeping My promise of blessing). So it looks like Abram could use a pep talk, and I give him a real beauty. I tell him once more that I Am going to keep My promise of an heir from his own seed, and then We up the ante again. I take him outside the tent on that clear night. And people, this is before internal combustion and industry, and the only pollution in the air is the little bit from wood fires, of which there are far too few to matter 50 miles south of Shechem. Everybody's fire is out this late at night anyway.

---

[36] Genesis 15 for what follows.

So nobody in your time has seen what Abram does in this moment, at least not with your naked eyes, even if you've gotten up in the mountains away from cities' lights and smog. Think of that, though – the starfield you've gotten to see at some point in the clearest, darkest place you've ever been. I tell Abram to look up into an even clearer, darker sky and then promise him he'll have as many descendents as there are stars in that sky spread out over him that night. What does Abram do when the creator of the stars makes such a promise to him? He believes Me.[37]

But for some reason, although Abram totally believes Me here at the promise of an heir through whom seeded descendents as numberless as the stars will come, when I promise him the land they're going to need[38] (following the thinking of people + land = a nation), Abram comes back with, "How can I be sure about this?"

So of all the covenants I make with humans (there was a quick one with Noah, by the way – the one that got you the rainbow), the covenant I make with Abram is the most important of all because all that follow flow from it. Abram and I cut a covenant[39] in which I commit Myself in a legal contract to both grow his descendants to be a great nation and then provide them enough land for the whole lot of them when the time comes. This is way past "cross My heart and hope to die," past swearing with My hand on My Book. It is something that is only going to happen a few times in all of history, and this is the Big Kahuna into which everything later connects.

This is pretty exciting stuff, but it's still of the "hurry up and wait" variety for Abram. The next chapter opens with a scene that makes clear that Sarai remains barren despite all the covenantal fireworks that just took place. Years pass, then she and Abram essentially decide, "If in the past ten years[40] God hasn't figured out a way to do this, he's not going to. We'd better help him out."

Here's the solution[41] they come up with to "help" Me keep My promise: Sarai has Abram marry her slave girl, Hagar. After all, they're in a polygamous

---

[37] Genesis 15:4–6 if you haven't gone over the whole scene already. It's yet another pivot point, so do look it up at some point along here.

[38] Genesis 15:7, remembering Lucy van Pelt's annual Christmas gift wish – real estate.

[39] Genesis 15:9–21. Walking between split animal halves conveys, "May the same be done to Me if I do not keep My vow promised at this moment." I mean, good luck with that, but I Am in earnest in making this vow.

[40] Genesis 16:3.

[41] Detailed in Genesis 16.

habitat, and Hagar's young and fertile. Abram is old but, well, able. Hagar conceives. Of course, when you've got two wives, one old, postmenopausal and barren before that, and the other young and obviously fertile with her growing belly and all in the same household, there's going to be a good deal of drama that comes into play with family jealousy and such. Sarai is so tough on Hagar, the young expectant mother runs away for a time, but I call her back with the promise that I have heard her cries in her misery. So when Hagar bears Abram a son, he gets Herman Melville's favorite name: Call Abram's son Ishmael, "God hears." We could spend a long time on him and his destiny,[42] but that's another story entirely. Abram is blessed with this first son at the age of 86, meaning it's been 11 long years since I promised him an heir through Sarai.

I'm not going to sit here and tell you that when you do things My way they're always going to be easy, or that they're going to happen right away; however, I Am going to tell you that when you do things *your* way instead of Mine – as Sarai and Abram just did, drawing innocent Hagar into their plot – there's certainly going to be extra, unnecessary drama, and not the pleasant kind. Better to just stick with Me, friend.

Well, they say time heals all wounds, and Sarai and Hagar certainly have some time to work on their relationship and smooth out that household drama, because the only changes that happen around their house for the next 13 years is the growing up of Ishmael.[43] Still no baby for Sarai. She and Abram are still waiting for Me to keep My promises, going on two decades now. I'm not waiting in order to punish them for trying to "help" Me. I'm not waiting in order to tease or play games with them. During this time, their trust in Me is incubating and growing, and with every year that passes and the more impossible it becomes for a couple of their age to conceive a child, the more clear it will be to all the world that their son, who of course is eventually going to come along – in My time – their son has his origins in My will, My purpose, and My doing.

But before that happens, I want to take things to the next level with Abram. God bless him, and I do, the old guy is a whopping 99 years old

---

[42] Genesis 16:12 sums it up.

[43] You have to do math with Abram's stated ages to see this. Thus, Ishmael quietly reaches his 13th year, the age which will eventually mark official "manhood" in TOM (even though many in your habitat wait until twenty years later to reach theirs). Ishmael has spent a full childhood of favor in Abram's home, despite Sarai's prejudice.

when I appear to him again[44] and remind him Whom he's dealing with: *El Shaddai*,[45] God Almighty Himself, or at least the most powerful deity Abram can wrap his mind around at the time. I essentially recap for Him the promises I've made already and affirm that they will be so: "Abram, if I say you're going to be the father of many nations, that's how it's going to be. In fact, I'm changing your name[46] from Abram (exalted father) to Abraham (father of a multitude) so that everyone who knows or hears of you will know of My promise to you." While We're at it, Sarai is renamed Sarah (princess), for at Abraham's side she will be the mother of nations and their kings.

And it's all going to happen through the offspring that I bring about. If you read Genesis 17 in any translation, they're again going to use the word descendants, offspring and generations to make nicer the word I use seven times[47] in My promises: seed, an unapologetic direct reference to the genetic material with which Abraham is going to impregnate his up-until-that-moment-barren wife. And the numbers of descendants that are going to burst at the seams into nations are going to come about in the same way, like it's been going on since Cain and Abel were conceived. All these conceptions of all these descendants are only possible because I Am keeping My promise to Abraham, so here at the beginning of that glorious sequence of promise-keeping and seed-passing and nation-begetting, I put in place a reminder that none of it would ever happen without Me. And that reminder has as direct a relationship as possible with the manner in which the promise is kept: circumcision. Not just Abraham, mind you, but all the males of his household, which include 13-year-old Ishmael as well as every male slave, have their foreskins cut off by Abraham that day. And there was weeping and gnashing of teeth.

This isn't an arbitrary act of mutilation, it is a sacred sign that all the life that passes through his marked gateway is a gift from Me. Belongs to Me, actually.[48] After calling Abram to step away from his family and country, this

---

[44] Genesis 17.

[45] This actually begins My quiet distancing Myself from the assumed Canaanite pantheon in Abram's thinking, and in his time, *Shaddai* has some geographic flavor to it in addition to the "Almighty" status it will later convey in total. We could add an entire chapter on the evolution of language and names across the years On The Way, so consider this and other footnotes like it a mercy.

[46] Like you knew I would.

[47] Genesis 17:7–12, 19.

[48] Also serving as an ongoing commentary and indictment against the various fertility "gods" who'll pepper the story throughout.

permanent action is a further setting-apart of Abraham and his family and an indication of My special involvement in and with their lives. Circumcision sets them apart from all other nations.[49] This very serious act, this sacred sign binds Us – Abraham, his family and Me – into a very serious, sacred relationship. With it, I Am bound to Abraham and his seed, and Abraham and his seed are bound to Me in covenant. As an added bonus (and as with a lot of My requirements) circumcision ends up having benefits with regard to health, significantly decreasing the risk of infection and other maladies in the long years before you discover antibacterial soap. Who knew?[50]

So Abraham and Sarah have got themselves fancy new names, and Abraham's got himself some remodeled old equipment, and they have been waiting a good long time – 25 years now – for it to be the right time for Me to fulfill My promise to them. My time is always the right time, and so at just the right time, they come together and Sarah conceives and bears[51] the long-awaited son of promise. Such a source of relief, joy,[52] and happiness is he, they name him Isaac, "He laughs."

Not so much on his eighth day, though, the day I set with Abraham for circumcision in future generations. Obviously, this timing derives its meaning from the opening account of creation: We worked for six days and whipped Us up a universe, then rested on the seventh. To set this seal of circumcision on the eighth day conveys a sense of a continuation of My work, but instead of working on My own as during that first set of days, the work is being done with and through humanity in the days that follow, beginning with the eighth day. Feel free to notice that a boy who's been around for eight days has been alive for one Sabbath, or that waiting that long gives him ample time to figure out the whole feeding thing and the comfort that activity will provide him, or any number of things that come together in this moment of covenant. When it is done as an act of faith (instead of simple hygiene) even today, it connects that boy all the way back to Abraham, all the way back to when he was just Abram stepping away from his daddy's tent for the first time. It connects him to My promises that every family on earth would be blessed through Abraham's seed. So, yes, there's a whole lot going on in that moment besides skin snipping.

---

[49] While a few of Abraham's neighbors practice circumcision, it's for markedly different purposes, done sometimes at puberty in order to promote fertility.
[50] I did.
[51] Genesis 21:1–7.
[52] Sarah even notes the comedic aspect of a newborn nursing at her withered breasts.

Now, you'd think I'd leave the happy family alone for a while, and in fact, I do. They've earned it. One last episode remains for them, though, and a tough one at that. Make that the toughest. You'll recall that Abram and Sarai had initially failed the test of time – faced with what they perceived as too long a delay in the fulfillment of My promises, they'd taken matters into their own hands and brought Hagar into the picture as a surrogate. What you could basically call cheating. Abraham has walked with Me for many years since that installment, though, and his trust and faith in Me has grown, especially when I was true to My word (which Abraham is still learning that I always Am, in spite of how long I take sometimes) when We brought Isaac along. But We had to know – both Abraham and I – that his faith had grown to the point of complete trust in Me – trusting in Me even when all appearances urged him to take matters into his own hands again.

I'll just go ahead and say it. I ask Abraham to kill his son, Isaac.[53] The son for whom Abraham and Sarah had waited for so long. The son through whom I said I would bless all humanity. It doesn't make any sense – to go through the years of waiting, having the promise seem to finally be fulfilled, and then cut it all short as some kind of cruel tease. It doesn't make any sense whatsoever when I ask Abraham to take his beloved boy on three days' journey from where they're staying and sacrifice Isaac to Me on a particular, seemingly random mountain. It doesn't make any sense that Abraham gets up early the next morning, rouses a couple slaves and his sleepy teenager,[54] and heads out with them toward the sacrificial site. It doesn't make any sense that their donkey is loaded up with firewood cut by Abraham himself earlier that morning so that he can offer up his pride and joy as a burnt offering to Me at the end of their journey. How could any of that make any sense at all?

Actually, it did make sense, at least to someone in that habitat. When people really needed their gods to come through for them – not just for a good crop, but in times of dire straights in terms of famine, enemies, or other emergencies – human sacrifice made a kind of twisted sense, the "you get what you pay for" kind. Herculean efforts required of your deity? Pay the highest price. What I Am promising Abraham – establishing nations through him and then blessing *every* nation through them – is magnitudes greater than anything anyone had ever asked for from any god, so asking

---

[53] Genesis 22:1–19.

[54] Isaac's age isn't given in the text, but he's got to be old enough to carry a big load of wood on his back, so let's put him at least in his mid to late teens.

him to pony up a human sacrifice in the form of Isaac in exchange fits the thinking of the time. It just seems like I Am shooting Myself in the anthropomorphized foot by requiring the life of the young man who was supposedly going to make it all happen. However, the fact that human sacrifice is relatively common in Abraham's habitat doesn't make it easy for him.

So, let Me tell you, these three days of walking with his precious boy beside him, with crematorial firewood riding on the donkey behind them, with the sharp slaughter knife hidden in the folds of his robe, are the longest three days of Abraham's life,[55] and hours feel like days for him. Finally, Abraham sees the place I want him to use for the dreaded deed – it's the highest place in the area. Of course, in Abraham's days, people think that the highest places on land are the best place to traffic with deities because mountain- and hill-tops are closest to Our heavenly places of residence. (Go up in a skyscraper that caters to tourists these days and you might run across a sign saying that "this is the closest to heaven some people will get," so you're still stuck in a "God is up there" mode of sorts.) Abram leaves the servants and donkey behind, piles the wood onto Isaac's strong back, and the two of them climb the hill.

I nearly call it then, watching Isaac with the firewood on top of his back, knowing it's about to be the other way around – with him laying on top the wood. Abraham carrying in his belt the knife he knows will dim the light in Isaac's eyes and forever silence his son's laughter – and Abraham's and Sarah's. The boy knows they're climbing the mountain to make a sacrifice. If it hadn't come up in three days of walking, at the very least his dad has just told the slaves they were headed up the hill to do so. Isaac's an observant young fellow, and when he asks his dad where the lamb is for the burnt offering, Abraham can barely choke out that I will provide the burnt offering Myself.[56]

They get to the top of the mountain – nothing like the Rockies, mind you, more of a hill compared to them, but still a hike – and build an altar out of nearby stones and arrange the wood on top.[57] Then, without a word, Isaac lets Abraham tie his arms and legs and lay him on top of the wood. Just as Abraham lifts his sharp knife to slit his own son's throat, the angel with My

[55] And the second longest three days in Mine.
[56] Genesis 22:8.
[57] I keep putting little nudges in, but now have to stop and say that you really ought to break TOM out and read this account in Genesis 22. It is one of the most important passages in My book.

clear instruction to intervene at just that moment stops Abraham from doing anything further. The relieved angel happily tells Abraham that, because of his faithful obedience, not only are all families going to be blessed through his family, but his descendants are going to outnumber both the stars and the sand on the seashore, a new level of numberlessness in the promise. A relieved Abraham happily spies the well-placed ram with his horns stuck in a nearby bush, and the ram takes Isaac's place in sacrifice. Whew.

Since he did not hold back even his most precious son from Me, it is clear to Me – and to Abraham – that his tested faith and trust in Me is complete. Oh, Me, so many lessons here. The lesson that I Am not like the gods of the nations: Although the other gods on the block may go for human sacrifice, I do not. (In fact, once We get a bona fide, codified law written down, that will be expressly forbidden.) That may seem like a no-brainer to you, but remember how early We Are at this point On The Way; I Am going to be helping people measure the distance between Me and the pantheon of habitat gods for a good while longer. People really have a hard time letting go of trusting in their own efforts, making bargains with their deities, and the-more-you-do-the-more-you-get, get-what-you-pay-for way of thinking. That's what child or human sacrifice amounts to: doing the most *you* can – or at least the most your victim can – in order to leverage the deity in focus to act in your desired manner. A way of giving you power over the god from whom you're asking help. Manipulating them, basically. It's a pervasive way of thinking, whether it's toned down into jumping through ethical performance hoops of religious activity aimed at forcing My hand, or up at full throttle à la Temple of Doom. Not Me.

Another lesson, and this is a big one, is that no matter what I ask of you, I will provide the way for you to do it. It may even seem impossible. It's okay if you feel like you don't have it in you, because you probably don't. I called Abraham past what he could do on his own, and because he believed and obeyed, an impossible son is able to wonder, "What the heck just happened here?" as that ram sizzles on the coals. So deep and strong is this lesson in Abraham's heart that day that he names that place "Yahveh Will Provide." I will never ask you to go anywhere, do anything, or become anyone that I Am not fully prepared and planning on providing the way for and through. And I'm never going to ask you to do something I'm not willing to do Myself.

There will be a lot of heroes in this story, but as far as the humans are concerned, not one of them holds a candle to Abraham in My Book. You see, it's not like he thinks Isaac is an annoying brat and can't be bothered to give the kid the time of day. Abraham is head over heels in love with that boy; yet when I tell him I need him to, Abraham is ready to give him up. His belief muscles have been strengthened enough across the years and miles that Abraham believes that I Am able to bring about the promised numberless nation even if Isaac is taken off the genealogy. Abraham believes that I can give him another son, if necessary, the same way I'd given him Isaac. That Abraham is willing to follow through and sacrifice his beloved boy proves to Abraham and to Us that his faith in Me could not be more complete. It's no accident that it's at this moment of fullest faith that Our fullest promises with regard to numberlessness are conveyed to Our champion.

The very reason Our promises to Abraham are able to reach their fullest is that his belief doesn't stay in one place. We noted he had a decent amount to start with, but *that* Abram was far from the old man walking back to his donkey with his son still intact now. It's through the long years of waiting that end in fulfilled hopes that he learns more about Me and about how much he can rely on Me. It's because Abraham was willing to let go of the known and the comfortable back in Ur that he and future generations will inherit a land in which to fulfill their destiny as the nation that carries forward all Our promises. It's because Abraham believes I can make him and Sarah what they can never become on their own – parents – that they finally become them. It's because Abraham hangs in there and stays the course that Isaac is finally born. Abraham is clearly human and not without flaw[58] by any means, but he perseveres for 25 years – up to the ripe, round age of 100 – trusting that I will come through. Think you're waiting a long time for something? Take courage from Abraham.

Finally, it's because Abraham is willing to let go of Isaac that he receives back from Me not only his son, but the exponential waves of generations of descendants that will follow. Because of all these things and more, Abraham and those who come after him in fulfillment of Our promises become the foundational means through whom We rescue humanity from the damage, brokenness, and destruction of sin. The Abraplan has begun.

And so We return to Our initial notice of Abraham. In spite of so crucial a role, he is less a superhero than an example of what a regular human being can accomplish when they trust in Me. Thus, his example is all laid out for you to follow in the ways We've noted across the chapter: answering the

---

[58] E.g., lying about Sarah to save his skin (when I would have anyhow), cheating on heir-making with Hagar, plus another lying episode in Genesis 20…

call away from the past and letting go of it; stepping out into the unknown and into Our call in faith; trusting in Us to reveal more On The Way; being faithful in what We've shown you already, and then in the greater things We show you farther along The Way; believing We can take you well beyond your natural self; hanging in there when it seems like We Are taking way too long to keep Our promises; and knowing that when We do keep them, it has all come at the right time.

You may already be able to look back and mark points of call We've made on your life, or perhaps this kind of thinking is a bit new to you. We have been working, whether you've noticed or not, but you wouldn't be reading still if you didn't have Me on your radar at least on some level at this point. One of the reasons We've called you to this volume is to help you see how much like you the people chosen for important roles along The Way are, just as this chapter started with all the regular people going about their business and getting listed in genealogies. Abraham is as unremarkable as the next fellow, neither a noble nor a captain of industry, clergy nor cleric. If anything, he and Sarah are considered less than normal by their habitat, yet it is through them that all nations will be blessed and rescued.

Abraham doesn't have to do the rescuing, and neither do you. I Am going to handle that end. Abraham simply has to believe, and then walk that belief out by acting like what I have promised is going to happen. I know you're up to that. We Are in this with you for the long haul. Abraham's thousand mile, twenty-five year journey clearly didn't happen all at once, but was walked out one day at a time. Just like yours, friend. As you ponder upon what to leave behind, and what to walk toward, remember that, like Abram, you aren't on your own. Focus on Our being with you on your walk On The Way today, on sensing Our presence, Our guidance, and Our promises. Abraham walked in the belief that I would do all I had promised. I Am still keeping those promises, to him and to you. Live in that certainty, friend. Decide to act in that assurance in matters great and small, and you'll be well On The Way with Abraham.

Chapter 8

Ike, Jake, and the Boys

As you can imagine, the whole Dad-nearly-slit-my-throat incident is a tough one to get over for Isaac (or "Ike," Our affectionate diminutive for him). Of course, Abraham fills him in on all Our prior conversations with him on their three days' journey home, but still. Not a single chat between them is recorded in the narrative of the remainder of Abraham's life, nor is there mention of them ever even being in the same room (or tent) together; and the choice words that sail out of Sarah in Abraham's general direction when she hears what they've been up to for a week certainly do not need to be recorded for all posterity.

Ike surely is given a great deal to think about at a tender age, and the quiet boy grows to be a deep thinking man. The next time he appears in Genesis, Isaac is taking a meditative evening stroll as a brooding 40-year-old with his own place, grieved at his mother's recent death.[1] In his sorrow,[2] Ike lifts his eyes from the field he's crossing and sees a group of camels headed his way, and they're loaded. In fact, they're carrying precious cargo indeed intended for Isaac: his wife, Rebekah.

Remember, this is not your habitat, so don't get upset at Abraham for picking out a wife for his son. You can also reign in any criticism that she's from amongst his cousins.[3] This not-marrying-gals-from-amongst-the-pagan-neighbors will be an important theme in choosing spouses as We go along, so the choice of Abraham's cousin Bethuel's daughter Becky (making her Ike's second cousin, in case you missed it) is a good one.

---

[1] In procuring a burial plot for her, Abraham owns his first piece of the Promised Land in Genesis 23.

[2] Genesis 24:64.

[3] Now is not the time to worry about the gene pool. It's still deep, and We're just getting started.

Well, it isn't actually Abraham who picks her, it's Abraham's trusted chief butler, the oldest servant in the now sprawling household. Well, it isn't exactly the servant's choice either. He has the good sense to leave the choice up to Me, but We're not going to go into that, at least any further.[4] Suffice it to say that Abraham has Jeeves[5] return to the old homeland to get a kissing cousin from amongst the family back there to be Ike's bride. This whole sequence raises one red flag after another in your habitat, but in Abraham and Isaac's time and culture, Abraham's just doing his job, and doing it well by his boy, and he will continue to do so. At his death in the relatively near future, Abraham will pass his entire sizeable estate on to Ike, to the exclusion of his various other issue – whom the old man had already substantially gifted so as to not leave them without resource.[6] So, thanks to Abraham, here come the cousin-laden camels.

And wouldn't you know? Isaac goes and marries his mother. Not that way, for Pete's sake. You married folks know what I'm talking about. A few years into your marriage, it hits you – the very trait that annoys you most about your opposite gender parent is right there in your mate, only you didn't notice it during the wine, roses or honeymoon. Though that analogy is not entirely fair to Becky, for I'm not talking about sharing an annoying personality trait with Sarah, though all of you have some of those. Rather, they share a physical condition: Rebekah too is barren. It takes 20 years of prayer before she's pregnant – less than her in-laws Abram and Sarai had to wait, but still enough to make a few things clear: that I Am the one making good on My promises to Abraham (and his seed, Isaac) in the offspring department; that the enormous family that's going to be erupting here pretty soon isn't because these folks come from a long line of überfertility; and that nothing like a little pre-existing medical condition is going to stand in Our way.

There's a whole lot that could be said about this happy foursome. You see, Rebekah bears Isaac twin conflicting boys. They're bashing each other's skulls even in the womb. You think *you*'ve been ready for a pregnancy to finish? Becky's got you beat, I guarantee it. She can't wait for the wrestling to move outside her abdomen, even asking Me, "Why is this happening to me?" at the peak of the boys' in-belly brawls.[7] At last, Esau's a swarthy red fellow who

---

[4] Though We heartily encourage you to read the whole account in chapter 24.
[5] Eliezer, actually, set earlier to inherit Abraham's estate if We didn't come up with the progeny promised (Genesis 15:2).
[6] Genesis 25:1–6.
[7] Genesis 25:22, within the full sequence of 25:19–27.

comes out first, but his twin Jacob is holding onto his heel, like he just barely lost their race to the birth canal. And they're about as different as they can be as they grow up. Outdoorsman Esau is a burly hunter favored by dad, and Jacob's a real momma's boy that hangs around the tents and learns how to cook.

There's all manner of intrigue a-swirl around Jake, all through his story, which you could tell was coming at his birth. I mean, who holds onto their brother's heel on their way out? Even his name – Jacob – means "heel grabber," and that instinct to position himself and manipulate circumstances to his own advantage runs strong in Jake. Might as well switch his name from Heel Grabber to Manipulator. Since he lost the birth race to Esau, Jake manipulates his way into the first-born heir's driver's seat by tricking first his brother and then their dad. The Manipulator's cooking skills come in mighty handy one day when Esau feels so famished, he impulsively sells his birthright for a bowl of stew, which is the full price Jacob exacts from his hungry brother.[8] Later, when their father Isaac is old and wants to pass his blessing onto his firstborn before it gets too late, Becky gets wind of it and determines to get her favorite son blessed instead.[9] She cooks up Isaac's favorite antelope stew, then helps Jacob convincingly masquerade as his older brother in order to capture the life-altering blessing. Dear old Ike suspects something's up, but bless him, his eyes are shot, and Becky has Jake wear his brother's clothes so he'll smell like Esau, and even straps goat skin to his hands and neck so he'll feel all hairy like their eldest too. Rebekah knows her man, and Isaac falls for it. Thinking he's holding his firstborn, gives a strong and noble blessing to The Manipulator.

Sure doesn't seem fair, does it? Of course not. Now, I'm not taking responsibility for Becky's or Jake's actions just because they're part of the story, but let Me put a couple things out here. One of the points of the story line with these boys is that My Plan is going to move forward on its own, regardless of cultural conventions. In the habitat these two are raised in, the firstborn pretty much gets everything when daddy dies, though other heirs get a little something.[10] It's that whole legacy thing going on – keep your line alive by giving your firstborn the best possible chance to make it with as many resources as possible. If I was going to strictly abide by this cultural convention in moving the Abraplan forward, you'd have been hearing about "The God of Abraham, Isaac, and Esau," but you've heard otherwise. Yes, I can use habitat norms just

---

[8]   Genesis 25:29–34. You'll never look at lentils again without thinking of Esau.

[9]   Genesis 27:1–29.

[10] As Abraham did with his other heirs in Genesis 25:5–6.

fine, like We do in bringing cousin Becky into the picture. I can just as easily move My purposes along when habitat norms get set aside, as I'll do with this family in bypassing the rough and impulsive older brother in favor of his wily sibling. Because of his mother's favoritism and his own conniving, Jacob is the one who receives the birthright and blessing from his father, the blessing that'll move Our covenant with Abraham forward as Isaac's words spoken over Jacob play out across generations:

> May God give you heaven's dew
>   and earth's richness—
>   an abundance of grain and new wine.
> May nations serve you
>   and peoples bow down to you.
> Be lord over your brothers,
>   and may the sons of your mother bow down to you.
> May those who curse you be cursed
>   and those who bless you be blessed.[11]

Provision, power, and protection – everything needed for the family vessel of the Abraplan to fulfill its appointed role, moving into the next generation via Jacob now instead of his firstborn – though it be by minutes – brother. Some would say I'm choosing the lesser of the evils I have to work with in those two, which would be fair, and another example that I'm using plain old people – scheming, warts and all – to work towards the goal. This is yet another piece of evidence that this isn't fiction – Jake would've surely been a much nicer fellow in the story if somebody was making all this up.

His flaws – and his mother's – are up front and center in this account, as will be true with most of the protagonists We come across with you. While We won't do this every time, each episode calls for a moment of prompting for you to do a little self check. You see, if We Are moving Our purposes forward through Becky and Jake in their time with and in spite of all their undesirable cheating traits, We can do the same with and through you, regardless of your major flaws. So many of you think you need to get your act together before you even make a move toward Me, much less consider yourself part of the team. To that, let Me say this: Please don't wait until you feel ready or deserving to step On The Way with Us. You're not ever going to have your act together, but

---

[11] Genesis 27:28–29.

We will bless you nonetheless, and empower you to play an important role in working out the Abraplan in your time, just as We Are doing with Jacob in his. Besides, We Are not yet finished with him, nor with you.

When it's time for Jake to get himself a wife, Ike departs from his own father's practice in a bit of rebellion – you'll recall that Abraham gave Isaac no say in the matter – and lets Jacob pick his own bride. Sort of. He sends the boy back to his grandpa's place up north (where Ike's mom Becky grew up), still avoiding local Canaanite girls who're worshipping the competition. I make it clear to Jacob that he's My next link in the Abraplan chain with a little encounter on the road to Haran,[12] where he's set to gain that wife. While he's stopped for the night and napping on a stone pillow, he sees a ladder reaching from earth to heaven, with angels hopping up and down it. Then I pop up next to him and basically pass the promises We made to his grandpa Abraham directly on to him. After introducing Myself as Yahveh, the God of His grandfather, Abraham, and his father, Isaac, I transfer the Abraplan promises and responsibilities directly onto Jacob's shoulders:

> I will give you and your descendants the land on which you are lying. Your descendants will be like the dust of the earth, and you will spread out to the west and to the east, to the north and to the south. All peoples on earth will be blessed through you and your offspring. I Am[13] with you and will watch over you wherever you go, and I will bring you back to this land. I will not leave you until I have done what I have promised you.[14]

We've already gone through all this when We first said it to Abraham, so at this point We'll just notice that, while Jacob certainly has heard of this promise from his father, the fact that I personally stand beside Jake and tell him that he's the next man in The Plan really lights him up. He awakens the next morning excited as he can be, turning his stone pillow on end as a pillar – the first ever pillow pillar – to mark My presence there. He names the place Bethel – house (Beth) of God (El). Not a fancy name, but one that points straight at Me. No matter that the place already has the name of Luz. All kinds of things and people get their names changed after

---

[12] Genesis 28:10–22.
[13] We will maintain our now long-settled practice of capitalizing the appearance of Our Name in English. We will have much more to say about it all in the next chapter.
[14] Genesis 28:13–15, if you didn't catch it in the full reference in the last footnote.

an encounter with the Almighty Me, and their name is often the least of the changes I bring.

So you'll have to pardon a quick side notice of parallels in your life here – in terms of Jacob's personal experience with Me creating an anchoring aha for him. Like you, he's heard about Me and My promises all his life, but he hasn't really thought through the fact that they include him. Now he knows. If you haven't realized it yet, this is not all just ancient history, but something that's still going on today: The terms of the Abraplan are still in force, still working their way out in Our relations with humans in current transformation and ultimate rescue. That plan is being carried out and passed on by pivotal people, and whether you think so yet or not, you're one of them; or at least, I Am calling you to be. One of the reasons I Am having you read this is for you to wake up one morning (on a much softer pillow) and realize you've heard My call as clearly as Jacob does here; realize that you too are pivotal in Our plan to transform and rescue all humanity. The Plan has shifted to a different phase in your time,[15] and your genealogy doesn't determine whether you're in or out – your choices do. Choose then, to hear My call to your pivotal role in the Abraplan. Yes, I want to rescue your blessed behind, but We also want you to be as real an agent of blessing as Jacob. Who, as We Are hitting you over the head with, is probably an even more unlikely candidate for such a role as you. So take courage, and take Our call.

We've established from before his birth that Jacob is a master Manipulator. As such, he shouldn't be surprised that his Uncle Laban pulls a fast one on him. Apparently, it runs in the family. Upon arrival in his uncle's neighborhood, Jacob has a "chance" meeting with his cousin, Rachel, and it's love at first sight. Jake agrees to earn the right to marry his beautiful cousin by working Laban's flocks for seven years. Jacob's so in love, seven years of life are a small price to pay for wedded bliss, and they pass quickly.

Now, it's poetic that someone who won his birthright with a tricky bowl of lentils should receive a bit of payback of the same firstborn flavor. Of course, Rachel is not Laban's oldest daughter. Leah is. Now, Rachel is said to have "had a lovely figure and was beautiful," but the only thing the writer can muster on

---

[15] You're welcome. And you can bet We will spend some good time unpacking the current phase in a later volume.

Leah's appearance is a brief reference to her eyes, meaning she wasn't easy on others'.[16] And if you don't already know what happens next, you can guess.

Wedding veils are sheer lacey afterthoughts in your habitat, but in Jacob's time, they're so thick that Harry Styles could be lurking beneath that veil across from you and you'd never know it (unless he started singing "Watermelon Sugar" under there).[17] Jacob thinks he's marrying his true love, Rachel, for whom he's gladly worked seven years. True to his habitat, though, Laban won't marry off his younger daughter, Rachel, before the first-born. With a slyness equal to his nephew's, the father of the bride switches in his older daughter, Leah, and Jacob marries her instead; something the groom somehow fails to notice until he and Leah have consummated their union. THAT honeymoon ends with the sunrise and the light it sheds on the situation.

Not really. Laban makes Jacob stay married to Leah – as in Leah alone – for the customary full honeymoon week, then Laban relents and lets Jake marry Rachel too. Naturally, Uncle Laban requires another seven years' labor from Jacob in exchange, which will seem like a bargain after his first seven years' wages. For good measure, both girls bring their own maids along with them to establish their new household with Jake, something else that will trigger further family resemblance in time.

After fourteen years of working for his father-in-law, Jake has nothing to show for it in terms of wealth, but he has got two wives battling for his affection. Rachel has his heart, but Leah has his children as We take pity on her as the clearly less favored of the two. As already seen in the previous two generations of Abraplan wives, Jake's beloved Rachel remains childless, in spite of spending extra bedtime with Jacob in comparison with Leah, who still manages to pop out four boys in a row,[18] conceiving practically whenever Jake so much as looks at her in their early years. You can bet Rachel gets sorer and sorer over it.

That's where the maids come in. Just as grandma Sarai offered Abram her maid, Hagar, as a wife to move the progeny along, barren Rachel enters the race by putting forth her maid, Bilhah, as her surrogate to be Jacob's third bride, and Bilhah bears two sons in quick succession.[19] Leah seems to be finished, so she

---

[16] Genesis 29:17, within the fuller context of 29:15–30 for the whole sequence.
[17] If you're too old and sheltered to know who Harry Styles is, then it could be Gomer Pyle under that veil, and you wouldn't know it unless he started singing "The Impossible Dream."
[18] Genesis 29:31–35. Your manual likely has footnotes defining their names: Reuben, Simeon, Levi, and Judah.
[19] Genesis 30:1–8, yielding Dan and Naphtali.

one-ups her rival by putting her own maid in the surrogate mix, and Zilpah comes up with two sons of her own by Jacob, bringing the grand total to 8.[20]

I want to point out a little detail in the drama at this point. First of all, can you imagine the jealousy ricocheting around that house at this point? Well, poor Rachel is at the bottom of the pecking order, beneath even her own maid because of her failure to produce any offspring – the same position Sarai had put herself in. But then Rachel gets wind that Leah's oldest boy, Reuben, has come across some mandrakes in his fieldwork. Now, don't run out and get yourself any, but it's thought at the time that mandrake root, known also as "the love plant," has aphrodisiac qualities that aid fertility. So, Rachel trades her night with Jacob that evening – yes, they've got a schedule – trades her night away to Leah for the mandrakes. Rachel takes things into her own hands instead of waiting for Me, thinking that maybe if she uses an herbal supplement she'll be able to conceive. Here We go again.

So Leah gets that night, and she needs no influence from mandrakes to conceive again. We take her off her fertility break, and Leah bears her husband three more kids again in quick succession.[21] Two more sons (Issachar and Zebulun, her fifth and sixth, Jake's ninth and tenth), and a daughter name Dinah, who will spend a good deal of time with someone in the kitchen blowing her horn someday. Feel free to see abundance for Leah where she has made no attempt to manipulate Us, in contrast to Rachel and her mandrakes.

So Jake's up to 11 kids now, but none of them by his most beloved bride, Rachel; and no, the mandrakes don't work. If it hasn't been made clear yet somehow, here's another instance where taking matters into your own hands instead of trusting in Mine fails. Or backfires. In Rachel's instance, enough effort and time have passed to once again make it clear that the only way she's going to conceive a child is if I make it happen for her. And so, once again, in saving-the-best-for-last splendor, I finally open[22] Rachel's womb, and she bears Jacob his most beloved son, Joseph. Yes, that Joseph. She also eventually bears him his twelfth and final son; however, like many women in many habitats before yours, Rachel dies in labor, knowing she is bearing her beloved Jacob another son, for the boy is breech and on his way out. So it is with her last breath that Rachel names her son Ben-oni, which means "son of my sorrow." This is far too bitter a reminder to Jacob of losing his most

---

[20] Genesis 30:9–13, bringing Gad and Asher.
[21] Genesis 30:14–21.
[22] Genesis 30:22.

cherished bride, so he switches his son's name to Benjamin, "son of my right hand" and calls this special boy My Right Hand Man for the rest of this life.[23]

We're going to have to skip over a good deal of drama if you're ever going to finish this book, so with Our apologies to the two scholars who are actually reading this, We'll just say that Jake and his sprawling family make a successful move away from his father-in-law's place with a generous amount of flocks and livestock. He'd crossed the Jordan on his way there to get a bride with nothing but a staff in his hand; now Jake leaves with 4 wives, a dozen kids (this was before Benjamin came along), and an avalanche of goats, sheep, camels, cows and donkeys to boot. He finally heads back to the land of Canaan, the region We'd told Abraham to move to, and Jake has a surprisingly happy reunion with his brother Esau, who's sporting his own burgeoning tribe, along the way.[24]

Jake's held on to some warm, fuzzy feelings about Bethel – the place with the pillow pillar, ladder and all – so he returns to settle there with his fresh, large family.[25] What better place to raise your twelve sons and their sister than where Me Almighty has promised to take care of you? I like Jacob's thinking, and on his return, change his name from Jacob (the trickster) to Isra-El a/k/a Israel. "El" is Me, if you haven't caught that yet. The "Isra-" part can be translated "strive," "fight," or "struggle."

Significance? You can look at it two ways, and have it both. This could be "struggles with God," Jacob struggling with Me (he and I actually do have an all-night wrestling match on his way home).[26] As in, up to now he's been wrangling things on his own, but now is going to aim his heart and efforts in My direction (though We're sure to have some differences of opinion). The other option would be "God struggles," as in Jake's wiles have gotten him pretty far; from this moment on, though, I Am on point to do the heavy lifting. These people are My family now, and I'm going to strive, fight, and struggle on their behalf. It's not like I haven't been using the drama all along – I'm very good at that; it's just that the drama's about to head south, or rather, southwest, to Egypt, where I Am going to really need to be holding the reigns in order to see the Abraplan through.

But before We head down there, let Us process a bit here. We've just spent a good deal of time focusing on the nocturnal drama of the four wives of Jacob

[23] Genesis 35:16–20.
[24] An exchange which rates nearly two full chapters – Genesis 32 and 33.
[25] I also urge him to do so in Genesis 35:1–15.
[26] Genesis 32:22–32.

and their resultant baker's dozen of children, running extremely high to sons. We Are not going to focus on any more bedroom antics like this in Our story (well, there will be that episode with… you'll see). This family calls for some scrutiny, though. Now, there are only five of you for whom this is going to be news, but it's still important to note this: Jacob's twelve boys are going to have families – large ones – of their own. Families that become the twelve tribes. We just changed his name, though, so they're not the twelve tribes of Jacob; they're the twelve tribes of Israel. That's got a nicer ring to it.

Once again, though, the noble sounding "twelve tribes of Israel" get their start as the offspring of jealous wives who in the very least are keeping track of who gets Jacob which night if not battling to bed him, then gloating over having the sons that issue nine months later; hardly a dignified setting, but a very human one. Once again, this exemplifies Our use of the ordinary and sometimes even the tawdry to further Our overarching purposes, and the life of each tribal namesake begins the same way every other life does.

Just now, though, those tribal heads are still mostly boys, though the eldest are young men. Now, in the grand arc of Our story with humanity, there are a handful of key people with whom We work in making things happen. A few are at the highest level in terms of moving Our purposes along – those with whom We enter a covenant, like Abraham. Call them Covenant Characters if you like alliteration, which works great with the next level of key players: Pivot People. Nice ring to that too, eh? You've heard Me mention Egypt so I'll wager you know which of these twelve boys I'm about to champion as a Pivot Person.[27] Once again, it's not going to be the firstborn, which would be Reuben. He's a sandwich, not a pivot. No, all of history and the moving forward of all My purposes will turn instead on the life and dreams of Rachel's firstborn, Jacob's beloved Joseph.

Joseph is special in his father's eyes, and in Mine as well. And as you can imagine, the intrigue and envy of the four wives vying for Jacob's attention over the years all gets imprinted onto the kids, and those boys are a jealous bunch. Take the time to read Genesis 37 to get the full rundown of what happens between them.[28] In terms of a big picture of the family's sibling

---

[27] Obviously, the fathers of the twelve tribes are pivotal, but not nearly to the extent that Joseph is. His role requires far more of him.

[28] Right this minute would be a good time to do that, or do the habitat thing and use your preferred video-on-demand service and watch *Joseph: King of Dreams* with a grain of salt tonight, whether you have kids or not.

atmosphere, think of Jacob's having made clear amongst his wives that Rachel's his favorite and how that must've gone over with the other three. Then have him not change much and unreservedly treat Joseph as his favorite son, feeding the fires of resentment amongst his older brothers. And, no, we're not going to talk about the coat.

We *are* going to talk about the dreams. Everybody has them, few remember them, and it's an extremely rare instance in which they make sense to anybody.[29] I Am with Joseph in a special way, and he has a unique double-barreled gift from Me – remembering *and* understanding those dreams that show the shape of the future. Unfortunately, he inherited his father's poor judgment in telling everyone everything he thinks, and relates to his older, stronger brothers that he's dreamed they will someday bow down to him. Well, you know what happens next: He's sold as a slave, headed to Egypt. (There is more to it than that. Reuben actually thinks he'll have the chance to sneak back later and save him if they just drop Joseph in a pit, but the others sell their brother without Reuben's knowledge. That's why you've never heard of a Simeon or Issachar Sandwich.)

It just so happens (wink, wink) that Joseph is purchased by the captain of Pharaoh's guard in Egypt: Potiphar.[30] Because I Am with Joseph, Potiphar can tell there is something different about the lad, and I bless whatever work Joseph lays his hands on. Before long, he's Potiphar's right hand man, and I bless the Egyptian for the trust he's placed in My son. We're talking more than your standard work-ethic-blessing here. Potiphar's trust is truly well-placed, for when the Egyptian's wife tries to bed the young, handsome Joseph whenever Potiphar's away, Joseph repeatedly declines, choosing to violate neither the trust of Potiphar nor of Me. So badly does she want him, she actually grabs him one day to drag him into bed, but he flees[31] her and gets out, though she holds on to his shirt as he rips away. Hell hath no fury like an eager adulteress scorned, and Potiphar's wife sees to it that Joseph pays for holding on to his integrity while she holds merely his tunic. With his stolen shirt as evidence, she frames Joseph for allegedly trying to bed her, the very thing she was after from the very beginning. Oh, the irony that lands Joseph behind the iron bars of an Egyptian prison!

---

[29] We will resist the temptation to bash Sigmund Freud at this point.

[30] Don't just take My word for it: Get the full skinny in Genesis 39 and those to follow.

[31] Joseph knew what few understand these days – sometimes you've got no other option but to remove yourself from a tempting situation. You may have one brewing yourself; if so, take a lesson from Joe and get out of Dodge. Don't flirt with sin. Flee it.

Even there, I Am with Joseph. First of all, this isn't the prison with the normal rabble of murderers and thieves; this is the prison where the king's prisoners are sent. Call it a low security prison of the white-collar crime variety (in your habitat – no collars of any color in theirs). As I did when he was serving Potiphar, I give Joseph favor in the sight of the warden, and before long, Joseph is literally running the place – and running it as well as he'd run Potiphar's estate. He moves about freely, making sure the prisoners are well cared for. As such, the other inmates hold him in the same high esteem as the warden does; rare indeed. A couple of the higher profile prisoners had served in the king's court[32] as his cupbearer and head baker; however, they'd each upset the king in one way or another, getting them tossed in the clinker. They could've just spilled wine on a new tunic, served white instead of red, put too much salt in the pastry, forgot how much the king hated fig filling, or some such minor infraction on a moody day.

Well, for the handful of you that don't know what happens next, after the cupbearer, baker, and candlestick maker are there awhile, these guys end up having dreams the same night. Even the nicest prison is boring, and a fresh story of any kind is highly welcome, so they chat their dreams up with the whole place the next morning, but nobody can make hide nor hair of them. Until Joseph makes his rounds.[33] Then comes My favorite part, where Joe tells them, "God's got the monopoly on interpreting dreams. I can tell you what He thinks if you'll tell them to me." And the cupbearer's dream about 3 grape-vines ends up meaning that, in 3 days, he'll be putting a glass of wine into the king's hands; in contrast, the baker's dream about 3 baskets with birds eating everything out the top one points to his certain demise in as many days, with the delightful detail of birds feasting on his flesh. Of course, they both come to pass, just as Joseph interprets them (according to My gift to him). But does the cupbearer[34] tell the king about it all and get Joseph hauled up out of prison? Nope. Could be he doesn't want to draw attention to himself just yet. Could be he just forgets. Could be it's just not time for that. Joseph needs to be kept in place close to Pharaoh's court until just the right time.

Let's stop a minute and notice that – notice Joseph's being stuck in an unpleasant situation, waiting for the next step – because this is a

---

[32] What do you call the king in Egypt? Pharaoh.

[33] Chapter 40 if you haven't been tracking along.

[34] The baker, of course, having been rendered permanently unable to relay Joseph's accuracy, at least verbally.

serious theme. Timing is everything, whether you're delivering a punch line or the human race. You could say that Joseph is a template in this regard. Although I Am blessing him and he is finding favor with the Egyptians – first with his owner, Potiphar, now with the warden – Joseph is still a slave. An imprisoned slave to boot. Not exactly what My breezy promises to Abraham sounded like. Believe it or not, We Are On The Way to making those things happen, and Joseph is a pivotal person in it. In order for him to play that pivotal role, though, he's got to be in this unpleasant place for longer than he'd like. We Are not punishing him by doing this. In fact, We Are honoring him in choosing him for such a role, though it seems a strange way to do so.

Your habitat has some pithy metaphors for having to go through a painful process in order to achieve a desired beneficial result. It would be far too crass, though, to sum up Our entire plan and journey with your race with "to make an omelet, you have to break a few eggs." People are not eggs, people. (Yes I know My biology – they *are* eggs, but that's *before* you're people, people!) Believe Me, you cannot imagine how intensely precious each one of you is to Me. Yes, I'm talking about you and Joseph at the same time. You're both My kids, and I'm just as crazy about you laying there in your pajamas, riding on your subway, whatever, as I Am about Joseph languishing there in Pharaoh's prison. He's there to move the Abraplan along at the right time. So are you. He's in the place he needs to be, unpleasant and less-than-ideal though it may seem at the moment, until the perfect time comes for him to move on. So are you. Did you hear that? I *know* you can relate to Joseph's current situation, My dear friend. Things are about to move forward for Joe, at just the right time, and they will for you too. When the time is right. So take a lesson from Joseph. He holds onto his hope, his faith *and* his integrity (no sex with Potiphar's wife, no prison embezzlement à la Shawshank); he holds on and hangs in there while he waits for things to move forward in what will be a unique opportunity that wouldn't have come without his time in prison. In fact, that time in prison is going to seal the fate of all of Egypt, Israel, and the very Abraplan itself. So We Are talking about the entire human race getting blessed out of those years in prison for Joseph. While the rescue of humanity may not always hang in the balance in the midst of your unpleasant circumstances, when the going gets tough for you, remember Joseph, and walk in his hopeful, faithful steps of integrity while you wait for the next chapter of life. It might be more important than you can imagine, and just a few pages away.

Speaking of chapters, let Us get back to this one. God bless Joseph (and you know I do), he spends two entire years bored out of his mind in prison until that cupbearer finally pipes up to the king about him. No surprise that Wine Man remembers Joseph's Me-given dream interpretation skills when Pharaoh has a doozy of a dream himself, or rather, a pair of doozies. A double doozy that none of his mystics can decipher. Well, whad'ya know? Enter Joseph into Pharaoh's court with perfect timing. After they shave his head, dress him up, and make him look like an Egyptian.[35] When Pharaoh tells him nobody can make head nor tail of his tales, Joseph again points to Me and tells the king he'll relay what I reveal. That's the way to do it, friend. Are you perhaps getting attention because of a gift I've given you? Make sure you know (and tell others) where you got that gift. And stop rolling your eyes when an athlete points to heaven after a noble achievement in acknowledgement of My having given them the ability to do so. You don't have to be showy about it, but that's the attitude We're talking about.

Now, I have given these dreams to Pharaoh. (Let Me just pause a moment and say that all dreams are not from Me. Sometimes Scrooge is right, and your dream is a product of an undigested bit of beef, or taking a handful of vitamins right at bedtime, or watching a disturbingly repulsive movie, or . . .) The dreams I've given to the king (scrawny cows and grains gobbling up their dreamy fat counterparts) give him fair warning of a coming seven year drought, a drought that'll be preceded by an equal term of abundance. Joseph relays this critical meaning, then puts forth a level-headed plan to be ready for the pending hardship: appoint a Famine Czar with his own team to squirrel away 20% of each year's crop in the fat years, then ration out the stores in the lean ones.

Pharaoh's no fool, and he knows that Joseph is speaking truth as soon as he hears it. The king knows *all* of it's true: Joseph's interpretation of the famine dreams *and* Joe's testimony that I Am the one behind his wisdom. It's clear to the king that I Am with Joseph, so Pharaoh goes all in. Not only does he make Joe the Famine Czar, Pharaoh makes him his own equal in every right except for who gets to sit at the head of the table at suppertime. And right on schedule, the abundance rolls in, and Joseph salts it away; then the famine arrives just as predicted, and thanks to Joseph and Me, Egypt is ready. Her neighbors aren't, though. Egypt quite literally has the corner on

---

[35] My apologies to those who are hearing Bangles right now.

grain before long, and when folks hear there's still bread in Pharaoh's land, they come from miles around.

Let's look at this a minute. Look at how I Am taking care of Egypt. Are they My Chosen People? Nope. I've entered into that exclusive contract with Abraham. Am I still blessing Egypt? Yep. Friend, I take no delight in the starvation of *any* child upon planet earth. Again, each and every one of you is My kid – then and now. Just as We've noted people in different roles as We go along here – some are Covenant Characters, others Pivot People, etc. – so entire peoples are cast in different roles across the ages. But just as Stanislavsky reminded you that "there are no small parts" onstage, there are no small parts in the drama of life, and We Are not working towards saving a single race in this grand plan – We Are working to rescue the *entire human* race. In this instance, I have blessed Egypt in order to care for all of My kids in their neck of the woods: She's the only one with the infrastructure to handle all the logistics of storing and distributing such huge amounts of food.

Thus, because I've used Joseph to prepare Egypt for the drought, she's the only source of grain in the region whose stores haven't run out. Others in the area may have set some food aside as a matter of course, just in case; but those stockpiles are of the meager rainy day variety, instead of the dry decade sort. So, just like some folks still ask their neighbors for a cup of sugar if they've run out, the neighbors come by asking for grain. And guess who comes a-knocking.

Well, to make a long story medium, Joseph's brothers head to Egypt for grain, and the family of Jacob a/k/a Israel is saved from starvation.[36] In the process, the brothers end up bowing before Joseph in fulfillment of his prophetic boyhood dream – both before they know he's their brother and afterward. Since things are so tough where they're living, and since Joseph is so favored by Pharaoh, the whole family moves to Egypt so their lives will be easier. Jacob nearly has a stroke when he finds out that the son he thought was dead – Joseph – is alive and well. Of course, I Am incapable of stroke Myself, but I know how he feels. Jacob really, really wants to see Joseph again before He dies, and there are still a good five years left in the famine. In addition, the taking up of residence in Egypt by the family of Jacob/Israel is an important step in the Abraplan (which of course We'll

---

[36] Because of its importance, this entire sequence involving Joseph as the vehicle for the family's move to Egypt covers the final dozen chapters of Genesis.

get to soon enough), so We give Jacob several thumbs up in a dream[37] On The Way there. Upon their arrival in Egypt, Pharaoh even lets them have the best available real estate – Goshen – where they're able to pasture their flocks. When he finds out they're shepherds, the king even extends them the trusting honor of looking after his own animals.[38] So Isaac's grandchildren are happily nestled into a comfy situation in Egypt in one big happy symbiotic relationship. For now . . .

[37] Genesis 46:1–7.
[38] Genesis 47:5–6.

Chapter 9
What's in a Name?

The first American Thanksgiving is held in 1621 at the Plymouth Plantation, and the Native Americans at the celebration outnumber the pilgrims nearly two to one. Relatively warm and fuzzy relations had grown up in the early months after the intrepid Mayflower discharged her passengers into a colder, harsher environment than they had anticipated. Helped by the kindness of Native Americans like Samoset, Squanto, and Massasoit, the foreign English are able to avoid certain death from starvation and instead establish a thriving colony. Peace pipes are smoked all round, and everyone recognizes how much they owe to their native helpers.

However, as you know, as time goes on, things change, and the settlers' view of Native Americans shifts drastically. Oh, those who celebrated that first Thanksgiving in 1621 – the 53 English who'd survived – never forget; but their story carries less and less weight with others in later generations. Eventually, instead of being seen as friends and allies, neighboring tribes are viewed as enemies who hold territory needed for expansion. Inexorably, that territory is taken away by settlers, their government, and its soldiers; and so the story goes across all of North America in cruel similarity.

And so it goes over three millennia earlier in Egypt. Though all of Egypt owes their survival to Joseph (and his trust in Me), and honor his large family as privileged guests as a result, there comes a time when these things matter no longer to a later powerful king of Egypt – a pharaoh who has no memory of Joseph, or at least acts like he doesn't. And so, instead of being seen as friends and allies, Egypt's Hebrew neighbors who'd come originally as honored guests are seen as enemies who might rise up against them unless they are put in their place. And that place into which Pharaoh puts them is slavery. Goshen changes from being a land of sanctuary into a prison.

Which should remind you of Joseph, how he was shanghaied by his brothers and ended up in prison, the place from which he would be called up in order to be the vehicle of survival for everyone in the region. Now the same thing is happening with his entire family, just as We said it would. Yes, this is not a pleasant situation, but it plays a crucial part in moving the Abraplan forward. Look back at what We said to Jacob about moving his whole clan to Egypt in Genesis 46:1-4. We're not going to tell you what it says this time – We want you to look it up yourself. Get TOM off the shelf or onto your screen, please.

Okay, it's right in there, isn't it? No cheating. Look at it yourself. What's going to happen[1] in Egypt? I'm going to transform Jacob's family into a great nation. I've already changed his name from Jacob to Israel. In Egypt, I'm going to change his offspring – those offspring that are all springing up from the seed of Abraham, passed on to Isaac, passed on to Jacob – from a family to a nationality. And how are We going to do this? Geometric multiplication.

Here it is: Once Jacob's family is safely nestled into Egypt's borders, they're off the food chain in terms of other countries coming after them. No predator nation is going to strike at Israel because they are covered by the protection of the biggest kid on the planet at the time: Egypt. And speaking of food chains, We've already established that Egypt is the best source of nutritional nourishment at the time. So the two greatest needs for any family – shelter and food – are covered, and covered abundantly, by Egypt. So it's only natural for the next human need – that of procreation, or at least its cause – to flourish there too.

As long as you've got your Bible out, turn a couple pages ahead to the front edge of Exodus. Go ahead and read the first chapter, because a whole lot hangs on what happens here. We'll wait for you. No really. Go ahead. Yes, I'm going to keep doing this until you read it for yourself. No, I can't force you – well, I could, but that's the thing about Us, We don't force anyone to do anything – but I Am asking very nicely. Would you please be so kind as to read the first chapter of the book of Exodus at this exact moment in time?

Thank you.[2] First, and We're not going to make a big deal out of this, but I'll bet you a hundred dollars that your translation is missing the first word of Exodus. It's "And." As in, "The story you think just ended with the

---

[1] Hint: verse 3!

[2] If you want to throw a little party tonight to celebrate finally getting out of the book of Genesis with Us, that wouldn't be entirely inappropriate. No party allowed, though, if you didn't just read Exodus 1.

final period of Genesis keeps on going here, so treat this more like the next chapter in the beautiful epic story of the Creator and His children instead of being some kind of separate tale just because we've switched from 'Genesis' to 'Exodus.' And by the way, the same principle will be at play for the rest of the whole book you're holding (i.e. the entire Bible and all the "books" within it to follow)." See? There's a whole lot in that "And," isn't there? So, if you've got an old-fashioned paper Bible you're reading from, go ahead and get out a pen and write the word "And" there right before it says "These are the names of Israel's boys…"

Then check out verse 7. The part about how fertile this big family is. That's a pivot sentence a lot of folks miss in Our story. Up till now, I've been making promises to make Abraham's offspring into a great nation, and We've been working with his family to that end. In this verse, they shift from being perceived as a family to being perceived as a nation, and their fertility is the key. You've already noted that the issue of fertility has been an important one for each generation thus far in the whole story. Sarah, Rebecca, and then Rachel are all born sterile and barren, then I heal each of their wombs and bless them each with children in fulfillment of My promises. You'll recall that this shows how clearly those promises are being fulfilled by My powerful, healing actions rather than by any human's ability to bear children. Well, now I'm doing for the whole family-turned-nation what I did for those three women. We're not talking everyone having a child or two. The words in the original Hebrew text that describe the Israelites' fertility are also used at times to describe a swarm of insects.[3] We're talking big families, friend. And they're going to be in Egypt a good, long while: four centuries. So that swarm of kids is growing up to have their own swarm of kids, who swarm their own offspring. Think about the numbers here. One couple who has, let's say, 8 kids, and those 8 have their own 8 – the "starter" couple produces 72 offspring in 2 generations. 72 out of 2 people. Multiply that by, well, a lot of couples to start with already, and then by a lot more than 2 generations in the course of 400 years. You get the point.

The midwives even testify to Pharaoh how hearty these Hebrew moms and kids are. I've taken the cursed edge[4] off birth for the moment and given them easy[5] labors; I've dialed their infant mortality and miscarriage rates down to zero, and lo and behold, time and math get together and produce an

---

[3] Exodus 1:12, 21.
[4] Genesis 3:16.
[5] Exodus 1:19. We'll be in Exodus for nearly all this chapter and will keep to our "numbers only" footnote practice.

exponential growth of these people. And because Egypt is providing shelter and food in abundance, it's an excellent incubator for nation-growing.

Now, I know some of you are obsessed with causality, as in, "Who gets the blame for everything we don't like?" And I'll admit, there's a lot to not like. Who wants to be a slave? Nobody. You're not ever going to get to the place, friend, where it all makes sense. I can say again that I know what you guys and gals are going to do – the choices you're going to make – and then incorporate them into Our plan (sometimes even when those choices are very bad and hurtful ones). That's about as human-friendly as the explanation gets, and it still leaves plenty to process.

Hear Me well. I hate slavery. I abhor it. I've been working toward its extermination for millennia.[6] I bring this issue up at this point because I want to help you see how Egypt's enslavement of Israel is not something I cause by any means. However, I'm still going to use the abhorrent (as I have used the ordinary and tawdry heretofore) in working toward fulfilling the Abraplan. Keep clear the fact that I don't reach into the new Pharaoh's memory and erase all the engrams concerning Joseph. He's the one who forgets, or handily chooses to forget, all on his own. It's *his* paranoia about how swarmy the Israelites are getting, and *his* fear of their turning on their Egyptian hosts that moves *him* to oppress the forgotten Joseph's clan.[7] But I know this king as well as I know any human, which would be thoroughly, and so We put his fears to use in moving forward. Ultimately, what that king intends as oppression for Our people will be the very thing that catapults them to nationhood.

So We've established why Egypt is the perfect place to grow Jacob's family into the nation of Israel. Shifting roles from guests to slaves, though obviously and terribly unpleasant, provides two additional essential things. First off, it keeps the Hebrews and Egyptians separate as races. Secondly, it highly motivates the Israelites to want to leave Egypt when the time comes.

Second point first. If things had carried on in the same relatively utopian state in which Israel's residence in Egypt had started, they would never want to leave. Leaving is crucial, because as part of the Abraplan to save humanity, his family-turned-nation has to exist on its own as a self-standing, land-holding entity. Not as a permanent guest of the big kid on the block. If things stayed

---

[6] I still Am. Google "International Justice Mission" and join Me.

[7] Joseph is another example of this as his nation tracks with his earlier destiny: I didn't throw Joseph in prison, Potiphar did; but you can bet your mummy I made use of the situation, even though I hadn't caused it.

rosy for them, and their families got bigger in number and girth, the promises We made their fathers would sound more and more theoretical as time went on. Instead, Pharaoh's decision to shift from the role of host to master of Israel will eventually light a fire under them so they'll want nothing more than to get out of Thebes. When the time comes, evacuation will be total and swift.

Now, race. When the Hebrews become the slaves of the Egyptians, it becomes inconceivable that anyone would marry across that impenetrable line. Again, before you get on your high habitat horse about My keeping races and countries separate, remember that We're taking the entire human race on a journey, friend. I assure you that The Plan has as one of its goals the permanent and final destruction of such barriers, and you can be certain that We'll process that in a while here. But for now, humanity isn't ready for that on multiple levels. And their sense of identity – especially Israel's sense of identity as the children and carriers of the Abraplan – has at its core the sense of being set apart for a special purpose. The Egyptian chapter of their lives is going to intensify that sense even more, which will in turn play an inestimably essential part in their maintaining their nation over the next umpteen hundred years in the face of nearly certain extermination and extinction. So We're taking the long view here, folks.

No marriage then between Egyptians and Hebrews. And the big theme of this whole episode snuck in a couple paragraphs ago. The part where Pharaoh decides to stop being Israel's host and start being their master. Excuse me, little fella, but I'm the only Master around here, especially when you're talking about My people. And when you start ordering people to kill My baby boys, you've declared war on the wrong Person, pal. As We go through this chapter, then, even when I'm not pointing it out, the theme of "Who's the real King here?" will be percolating. You know the answer.

And as long as We Are talking about themes, the last one I want to throw out there before We dip into the sequence of events again is the theme of water. We talked about it in the very beginning of Our chat – water is life. It can also bring death. For obvious reasons, it is a symbol of becoming clean; but We're adding a layer to that cleanness with this part of the story. Water is going to be the vehicle for salvation in Egypt – at both the beginning and end of this episode; and that powerful combination of cleanness and salvation is going to reach all the way through to Life On The Way in your habitat and time as well. But We'll get to that poetic connection a bit further down the pike. At this point, We've got to get little Moses into the story, or We're going to wallow in theory and hypotheticals until the cows come home.

Back to the narrative then. Pharaoh's already enslaved Joseph's family, and Egypt is putting them to harsh work. In spite of how poorly these folks are treated all day and as tired as they must be at night, I make sure they've still got enough bedtime energy for a little baby making. The swarms of Hebrew babies that keep on coming really freak out the Egyptian king, so he makes his second move (the first having been slavery): He orders the Hebrew midwives to kill all the baby boys at birth. As mentioned, this really riles Me. How in My green earth could it not? Those midwives are good people, though; they're My people, and they're more concerned with honoring Me than Pharaoh (Who's the real Master here, remember?), so they ignore him and let the boys live. Of course, when the small bald kinglet (My affectionate term for Pharaoh) calls them on this, the midwives report that the Hebrew moms are simply sturdier than their Egyptian counterparts. They're popping their kids out quicker than a colorful metaphor over in Goshen, and are all finished before the midwives can even get to them.

Well, Pharaoh's face is the color of a florid sunrise as he gives his next order, not just to midwives, but "to all his people: Every Hebrew boy that is born you must throw into the Nile, but let every girl live."[8] The boys will drown and likely be eaten by crocodiles, a terrifying prospect; many of the girls that survive will eventually wish otherwise as they are put to use by Egyptian men. When you're tempted to think that I treat the small bald kinglet harshly later on, remember these things.

And so water enters the story again and is the vehicle for death at Pharaoh's command of many of My sons, but even in the midst of such horrific tragedy, the river Nile also carries Our vehicle of salvation upon it: Moses.

Moses' mother, Jochebel, is a woman of wiles close to My heart and has the chutzpah to put her good-looking boy in a tar-bottomed basket before she takes him to the river and (gently) drops him in the water.[9] So she's obeying Pharaoh's command to put her baby boy in the river, but with her own modifications. That way her back is covered if she's caught: "Officer, I put my son in the river just as I was told to do. No one ever said to *not* put him in a basket first." Love that gal.[10]

---

[8] Exodus 1:22.
[9] Take your pick: Al Green's original, or covers by Talking Heads, Kaleida, The Commitments, Annie Lennox, Foghat (!!), Bryan Ferry, Levon Helm, Courtney Love...
[10] We recommend reading Exodus 2 at this point, which quickly covers the ground We're on.

Since Moses is Our vehicle of salvation for Our people (and as you'll see, for all people), the basket in which Moses-the-salvation-vehicle rides is an exceedingly rare means of transportation; it's very much similar in symbol and purpose to the ark of Noah a while back. Of course, Noah's waterborne vehicle was a good bit larger, but it too saved him from certain death in the water and made it possible for him and his family to reboot the whole human race. I'm pretty much doing the same thing here with Moses, only with a lot more style and a lot less animal manure.

The boy's not in the Nile long enough to even get on the crocodiles' radar. Jochebel has watched the river for many days and knows the princess' schedule like the back of her calloused Hebrew hand. She puts the basket in the water at just the right place, at just the right time to not be seen herself but still ensure the basket's notice by Pharaoh's daughter when she comes to the river for her daily bath. Jochebel does not put her precious boy out in the open water where the current could carry it away. She nestles his basket in the reeds where a crocodile might be hiding (of course, she makes sure there are no large reptiles in the vicinity first). You see, she knows that when the Egyptian princess is about to get into the river to bathe, the surrounding reeds are first all checked for crocs to prevent a royal dinner in the wrong direction. One of her handmaidens who's done the crocs-in-the-reeds check reports to Pharaoh's daughter that, not only are the surrounding reeds devoid of carnivores, but (quelle surprise) there's a basket nestled in them nearby; and the rest, as they say, is history.

Our favorite part of this section of the story is that Pharaoh's daughter actually hires Moses' mom to be his wet nurse – pays Jochebel to breastfeed her own son (remember, there's no baby formula in this habitat, folks), which his mother does until he's weaned.[11] This is handily brokered by Moses' older sister, Miriam, who pops out of her hiding place as soon she sees the princess take a liking to the understandably cranky boy. Miriam takes Moses home with a handful of coins, ransomed from the Nile with a new lease on life. Jochebel cherishes those next short years with Moses until he no longer drinks from her breasts. Then, like a mother sending a child to the boarding school she knows will bring a much better life than the one possible at home, she surrenders her boy into the arms of Pharaoh's daughter to be raised not as a Hebrew, but as a son of Egypt.

---

[11] Exodus 2:9.

Now, all through this entire chapter, I know a whole slew of you are going to be picturing Cecil B. DeMille's epic movie, *The Ten Commandments.* [12] There's no helping it, and it's mostly a good boost to your limited imaginations, though at 6′3″, Charlton Heston is a good deal taller than Moses, I can tell you that. If you've even glanced at the book of Exodus, you already know that a great swath of editorial license is taken with the story by Cecil.[13] I'm not going to pick it apart – it's a movie, for Pete's sake, and not worth the energy. One of the things DeMille does is to make a big deal about Moses not knowing he's a Hebrew until Anne Baxter spills the favas in explaining why she has to murder Dame Judith Anderson to protect his secret identity. It may make for good movie making, but search The Owner's Manual and you'll find no indication that Moses' dual citizenship is a secret to him, or that it isn't. In another example of sparse information in the need-to-know category, all Cecil or anyone else has to go on in Exodus' account of Moses' childhood is the acknowledgment that he has one, "One day, after Moses had grown up, he went out..."[14]

Surely you don't need a spoiler alert here, do you? If so, drop everything and read the first two chapters of Exodus immediately; because Moses is going to go out and kill an Egyptian for beating a Hebrew here in a little bit, and it's going to come pretty much out of the blue. Whatever has gone on in Moses' growing up to this point, he is certainly aware of his double identity now.

There is obviously a decided duality about Moses from the very beginning: an Egyptian *and* a Hebrew mom, and (wouldn't you know?) a name that has meaning in both languages. The Exodus text links the name "Moses" with the Hebrew word for drawing something out – a baby out of a river, a people out of their slavery. We just love that double layer there. So I guess We have to talk about at least quadruple name meaning for Moses, because in the Egyptian language, "Moses" and its derivatives convey a sense of being "the son of" whatever's in front of it, name wise, that is. Mostly gods. In Egypt, their alleged gods are popular namesakes for the kings, who fancy themselves as divine, so they name their boys things like "son of Thoth" – *Thutmose* – or "son of Ra" – *Ramoses*. So Moses gets a "son of" suffix as his name, but with the name of neither god nor man

---

[12] If you're over forty or a film buff, that is; half of you youngsters are instead hearing Val Kilmer and Ralph Fiennes sparring with one another in a cartoon. If none of this makes sense because you've not seen DeMille's epic, now's a good time to order it as decent imagination fuel.

[13] Don't even get Us started on Edward G. Robinson and Vincent Price. Oy.

[14] Exodus 2:11.

to indicate his source. Thus, Moses' name indicates to Egypt that he is the son of no one in particular, an identity crisis just waiting to happen. He's My son, of course, but I haven't told anyone My Name yet, so that part has to be left blank. Which just adds to the theological weight being freighted by this quick little name.

And as long as We Are talking about names, check out the Exodus text and you'll find that the name is never given for a very major player, the person second only to Me and Moses in importance: third, you could say. Actually, a couple major players, but they're literally closely related. Go ahead, see if you can figure it out. Got it? Of course you do, you clever reader, you. Pharaoh is unnamed and will remain so throughout to underscore his puniness in comparison with the Real King.[15] Even the midwives, pretty much the lowliest characters in the whole Egypt sequence, get their names included,[16] highlighting Pharaoh's ultimate insignificance in the face of My sovereign rule. Of course, there'll be some dramatic interactions before We're through to underscore the point, but the quiet absence of any name other than his function (remember, "Pharaoh" simply means "king"), is a tacit reminder of just Who rules whom here.

This brings up again a facet to this tale I mentioned earlier. This whole story and how it's told is a reminder that lots of your questions are going to be left unanswered for now. Why do you think Cecil had to make up so much additional story line to make that movie of his? There's precious little detail in the Exodus account, which is written like the rest of My book – on a need-to-know basis. If it's not in it, you don't need it! As a result, a lot is left unsaid. Imagine how long and heavy your paper Bible codex would be if, in addition to the things you *need* to know, the Scriptures included details just to set a more colorful scene or satisfy your curiosity? Wouldn't you like to know what Moses studied as he grew up in the palace? How he was treated by the rest of the royal family? Whether they all ate supper together at a big long table every night? All that part of his life is summed up with a simple sentence, "She took him to Pharaoh's daughter and he became her son."[17] That's it. The rest is all up to your imagination. And Cecil's.

---

[15] If you don't know by now that I Am talking about Myself as Real King, you haven't been paying attention.

[16] Shiphrah and Puah, sure to be the only one in her class if you name your baby daughter after one of them.

[17] Exodus 2:10.

It's safe to assume, though, that growing up in the palace as the grandson of Pharaoh has its perks for Moses, and his education is of the very top shelf variety, covering all manner of Egyptian history, language, and practice. Yes, Moses walks like an Egyptian, as well as reads, writes and reasons like one. So by his placement in that basket at just the right time, he is placed beside the sons of Pharaoh with their tutors in the Palace Homeschool, and becomes their peer on every level. This will be a quiet truth underlying My choosing him for the special mission We all know is coming.

By definition and design, life in the palace is sheltered from the impact of life in the world outside its walls. Other than his interaction with the palace servants – who have the most treasured positions of all the Hebrews – Moses is shielded in large part from fully witnessing the harsh treatment of his Hebrew countrymen at the hands of his Egyptian countrymen. However, once he grows to manhood and leaves behind the tutors and restraints of childhood, Moses is loosed from the palace confines and able to take in a broader survey of his two worlds.

So here he is, all grown up, and Moses does what any grown man of the family would do – he heads out to the great construction projects to see how the latest structure is progressing. Every Pharaoh has their own Preserve My [Biblically unlisted] Name in Stone agenda, and their Hebrew slaves are the ones building those edifices. What the Egyptians call progress, the Hebrews call hard labor; hard labor unlike any work you've ever done, friend, no matter how it may have felt at the time. All you have to do is take a look at what's still standing in your time right now over in Egypt – the temples, monuments, pyramids and statuary of Cairo and Luxor – and ponder the labor required to produce them – without power tools – not to mention all the structures that have lost their battle with sand and time; and you've got the beginnings of an indication of how hard the "hard labor" of the Hebrews is in Egypt.

Moses has been hearing stories about the greatness of Egypt, recorded and embodied in obelisks and the great building works long-completed within and near the palace. Up until now, he has measured the statues, pylons and walls with a ruler, and counted their bricks to tally their cost; but now, seeing such monumental undertakings in progress, he sees the real cost of these things is paid by the sweat and blood of the Hebrew slaves. As if it hadn't ever crossed his mind before, when he sees an Egyptian beating a slave, Moses is so enraged that he kills the Egyptian on the spot. It sure seems like he is surprised at witnessing this – for any number of untold reasons[18] – because he barely has enough presence of mind to check for witnesses and then quickly bury the body in the sand. The topic of how to hide corpses well apparently wasn't covered by his tutors, and the dead Egyptian isn't covered by the sand for long, so the story might as well have been in the morning papyrus.

Obviously, Moses doesn't think his impulsive actions through; though he believes that, in the very least, killing one of their oppressors will score Moses some major points with his Hebrew nation. "This'll make me the hero of the slaves!" he thinks. It's a moment that very much cements an "us versus them" thinking for him, and draws his "us" identity fully to the Hebrew side of the Nile. So when he catches two Israelites in a fistfight the next morning, for starters, it kind of puzzles him: "Don't these guys realize they're on the same team, and the enemy is Egypt, not another Hebrew?" Of course, you know what they say when Moses confronts them. "You gonna kill us too like that Egyptian yesterday?" They trust Moses about as much as they trust Pharaoh, but their question clues Moses into the fact that his dirty deed is common knowledge all the way up and down the social ladder.[19]

Knowing as much as he does about Pharaoh, Moses skips town faster than you can say Hatshepsut to avoid capture and death.[20] Knowing as much as he does about how far the hand of Egypt can reach, Moses travels far, far away to the remote wilderness of Midian. Where he finds himself pretty much as far as he can possibly get from the palace on every level. Which seems to be the wrong place for the one who'd been perfectly poised to straddle two worlds and negotiate some kind of deal between Pharaoh and the slaves. Well, until that whole murder-an-Egyptian incident.

So once again, consequence rears its ugly head in Our narrative and plays a vital role. Moses' presence in the wilderness of Midian is a direct consequence precipitated by his murder of the Egyptian; an action completely done on his own – We certainly didn't put him up to it. But you know what? It's going to come in handy after all. You'd almost think We planned things this way (but once again, I knew Moses was going to make that murderous decision, so made things work with it); because in spite of all he is and may

---

[18] The two that make the most sense are either that he's not witnessed such brutality before in his sheltered palace life, or that he's only recently been made aware of his Hebrew background. Some prefer the former, Cecil likes the latter. Which it is doesn't matter.

[19] All this and more is packed into that second chapter you haven't read yet.

[20] Cecil wanted a more colorful exit at this point, hence all his added banishment drama. Exodus 2:15 has Moses flee the admittedly roiled royal under his own power.

already know as a "royal family member," Moses is nowhere near ready to serve as the deliverer of My people. The only deliverance he's capable of at this point is to chase off some bullies at Midian who aren't letting the local shepherd girls get water for their flock.

As far as Moses is concerned at this point, he's just forced himself into a life of exile and will live the life of a fugitive outside the kingdom of Egypt for the rest of his days. As far as We're concerned, this is Our time to quietly work on Moses' heart. Before you can say "Jethro's my new father-in-law," Moses marries one of those shepherd girls, and takes up her humble trade alongside her. Away from the stone halls of Egypt and the great affairs of state, living instead a life bound to the cadence of nature in land and weather, no longer insulated and pampered, but grappling with life day in and day out; Moses changes in the wilderness. It's easy to feel strong and trust in yourself when you've always been told how great you are, when the examples of manhood to whom you look up are chiseled in stone and unquestioned in their rule and command; but then, in stark contrast, it's easy to feel how powerless and at the mercy of things beyond your control you are when there's nothing but an animal skin tent between you and whatever We Are sending out of the sky, be it sun, rain, or hail. Moses is humbled over the course of forty years. The puzzle of his identity wears away to reveal simply a man – nothing more, nothing less – a man with a family, a flock, and a God.

Now, before We go any further, let's think about an aspect to this that has some parallel in your life. Moses is now far removed from the situation at which his entire life seemed to have been pointed. It sure looks like his "destiny" has jumped the tracks. You too have had a similar experience to this, in terms of finding yourself catapulted away from something you were certain was headed your way, be it a relationship, a career, or whatever your definition of "the good life" may have been. It seems to be right there in front of you; then, bam, it's gone, or rather, you're gone – you're suddenly in the wilderness as a consequence of something you or someone else has done or decided.

As you can see in Moses, and as will become more apparent, the wilderness is an important and necessary time for him. Out away from the demands and distractions of "destiny," We can get downright simple with this beloved son of Ours and speak a quiet language into his soul – into your soul – that could never be heard in the cacophony of destiny. His heart had been full of himself and his assumptions, quickly as they were made; but in the wilderness, his heart – and yours – can be emptied of the things that crowd its limited space and leave no room for Us. Remember, friend, there is an empty place in every human heart left bare by your being torn from Us as a consequence of sin. Moses needs to learn the same lesson that you do – to set himself aside, to learn to reach out to Me, to trust in Me. Oh, he had it so much harder than you. In fact, as you think about him in what's about to happen, think of Moses as paving the way for you to come near to Me. He is heading into territory where no one has yet had the chance to tread, so to speak.

Now, if you've not spent much time around sheep, then let Me tell you, those critters are eating machines. They're My little organic lawnmowers. One sheep can tear through nearly a thousand square feet of grass per day – a goat will inhale nearly double that! So one of the first rules of shepherding is to keep your flock on the move so the grass'll grow back, so they can come back someday and eat it again, so you can move them on, so… it's one of the beautiful circles of life. Moses has been walking that circle for a good forty years now, and he's a different man than the one that showed up at the Midian watering hole decades ago – back when those shepherd girls ran and told their daddy that some Egyptian had rescued them from bullies. However, no one would mistake Moses for a son of Pharaoh at this point. He looks, walks, smells, thinks and feels like a shepherd. That's right. Thanks to his time in the wilderness, Moses now has within him the heart of a shepherd. What do you know?

When the temperature heats up in Midian, the grass is greener and thicker in higher altitudes, so shepherd Moses brings his flock beside what's known to be a hangout of Mine at the time – Mount Horeb.[21] Now, We're going to have a whole lot to say eventually about where We Are, and it's not going to be just on the tops of a handful of mountains. But remember, We Are in a long and deliberate process with the human race here, and right now (and for a long time to come), where We Are is assumed by Moses' contemporaries to be in a single place (no omni-presence, nor omni-anything, yet), and that place is almost always up. So the highest places in the neighborhood are assumed to be the likeliest places to find Us.

One doesn't have to be omniscient to know this would be where to find Moses at this time of year: This is his regular spot, and he's been coming here for decades. He knows the place like the back of his hand. So do I, and it's the perfect secluded spot for a chat.

---

[21] We Are finally crossing into Exodus 3 if you're one of the dozen actually tracking with a Manual beside you. Good on you, friend!

I Am particularly proud of how We get Moses' attention. We could've used all kinds of stuff – earthquake, meteor, lightning bolt, talking sheep, goats in a kick line singing, "There's no business like show business" in Ethel Merman's voice…[22] Regardless, it could've been big. It won't be long before I'm pulling pillars of clouds and fire out of thin air. It could've been something to put the fear of Me in the man; but no, We go for the understated approach this time, and just light up a bush. An ordinary, unremarkable specimen of common shrubbery, dazzling with the flame of My presence. It doesn't burn up – that's the heart of the metaphor here, folks. The bush is simply the vessel for My power and presence – a conduit, if you will. Just like Moses is about to be. Like you can be. At the beginning of the story, if he were a bush, he'd have burned himself out since it was all about him and what he could do. From his time in the wilderness, though, Moses knows how ordinary and small he is, so he can finally become the vessel for My strength.

So Moses catches sight of this slightly freakish phenomenon and comes over to check it out. You think he's surprised to see a bush on fire that isn't falling apart. You should've seen his face when My voice comes out of it, "Moses! Moses!" He'd have been less shocked to hear one of the sheep singing, "Nessun dorma!"[23] But he's seen a lot in the wilderness, and it takes more than a talking bush to totally ruffle his feathers, so Moses has the presence of mind to reply, "Here I am."

First words and last words are of particular importance, friend. First impression, final thought, both are emphasized in relationship and literature. Key in, then, on My first words to Moses, "Take your shoes off." This is not a suggestion like the Beverly Hillbillies' to set a spell. This is "because I Am here, this ground is holy, so behave with great reverence." Though it conveys the opposite message of casual familiarity in your habitat,[24] removing one's footwear in someone's presence is a sign of reverence in Moses'. We could go into the implicit meaning of removing whatever barriers there may be between you and Us, but We've got enough holy ground to cover as it is. I'd point out that Moses' first words in the conversation, "Here I am," hold the promise of open willingness to what I have to say, but he'll prove himself otherwise soon enough.

---

[22] Actually, that last one is more in the dark side's way of doing things.

[23] Google it if you don't know it, or even if you do. It'll make your day.

[24] Except in the homes of those who make their guests go shoeless, which is not about respect, but obsessive compulsion.

Not to belabor the point, but, as it proved so important at the outset, My holiness is going to be a substantial theme again here for a long time – well, pretty much for forever. If you can put a pin in this moment in your memory and hang onto it, it'll be a touchstone to which We return often. For now, I just want to capture this first moment with Moses in which the first thing he hears from Me, other than My calling his name - and there's a whole another chapter right there – is a declaration of My holiness.

Then I identify Myself, "I'm the God of your father." To be sure he knows I'm talking about his Hebrew dad, Amram (Jochebel's husband),[25] I continue with "the God of Abraham, the God of Isaac, the God of Jacob." In case you thought there's any chance Ra is in the vicinity. Knowing it's Me, though, Moses hides his face, afraid to look at Me; another sign of reverence.[26]

Well, things are off to a good start. Forty years ago, Moses might've started an argument with Me right away. Now he has the respect and good sense to wait a bit. I can't begin to tell you how much I've been looking forward to this moment. The moment when the time spent by Jacob's family in the nation-building incubator has yielded the great numbers they now possess as a nation. The moment when events can finally be put in motion to get My precious children out of their misery and into the next step in the Abraplan – the fun part where they have their own land flowing with milk and honey, wine and roses. Of course, We Are so very much not there yet, but this hillside conversation with Moses gets Us on the path, or rather, gets him and them on the path. We never left it. I say as much to him as I tell him I'm sending him on the mission to bring Our people – the enslaved descendants of Abraham – all out of Egypt.

That's when Moses finds his voice, as the humbling impact of his time in the wilderness is borne out. It is the shepherd who speaks, not the former prince of Egypt: "Who, me? Of what use could I possibly be?" Forty years ago, upon hearing My intention to liberate My people, Moses would have jumped at the chance and been halfway to Pharaoh by sundown, drafting Bedouins and total strangers into a ragtag army along the way. Working on his own juice, that is. Remember the bush: used but not consumed because it serves as a vessel for power that comes from Me. Moses is right there. "Moses, I will be with you. I will be the One that makes it all happen. And

---

[25] Though Amram's not named here, it's his big moment, all set up for him in Exodus 6:20.
[26] There are still several habitats in your time in which eye contact with a superior is a sign of *dis*respect.

it will be so clear that I have done these things – not you – that when I'm through, the only thing left for the people to do will be to come here and worship Me."[27]

Moses can remember the last time he chatted with another Hebrew – those two guys duking it out that last day in Egypt – and how little respect they had for him then. Thinking there's no reason for that to have changed, he knows his credibility is going to be an issue with the Hebrews (and the Egyptians, for that matter, but let's deal with one nation at a time), so he says, "Suppose I do head down there and tell the Hebrews that the God of their fathers has sent me, and they say, 'Oh yeah? Prove it. What's his name?'"

It's a bit along the lines of "What's the password for this level of security clearance?" He's asking for a password, but what Moses gets from Me is a revelation. I give My Name to a human being for the first and only time in history. Well, of course, I only have to give it once. Moses tells everybody after that.[28] Just like celebrities that don't have to introduce themselves, from this point on, (almost) everybody knows Who I Am.

And you caught it right there, didn't you? I tell Moses My Name is "I Am Who I Am". Kind of. The grammar isn't as simple in Hebrew as it is in your first person conjugation of the verb "to be," and what I say to Moses in Hebrew could mean several things. For you grammar nerds, it's a three word name, with first person imperfect as the first and third word, with a word that functions as adjective or pronoun in the middle; thus, My Name has three parts (another three, folks!) in ABA form. In plainer English, this "I Am" in Hebrew also conveys "I Was," and "I Will Be" at the same time. Then there's that "Who" in the middle, making My Name a "Who sandwich," something one might expect the Grinch to snack on. But that word in Hebrew is also flexible in its meaning and dependent on context. "What" or "That" are as likely as "Who." My Name could easily mean "I Am What I Am." And now all of you over 50 picture Popeye the Sailor Man, an unfortunate association. When I say it could mean "I Will Be What I Will Be," then the same age group hears Doris Day singing *Que Sera, Sera* in the background.

There's a whole lot packed into those three words, and here's what I want to get across in them. First, My Name is a declaration that I exist.

---

[27] We Are still tracking with Exodus 3, crossing 3:12 now.
[28] Since the ground We've covered thus far in TOM is all written down after I've had this chat with Moses, My Name is projected back into those texts. In case you were wondering, I know that opens up a can of mystery. Enjoy.

In a sense, everyone's name does that, but not as literally as using a form of "to be" as One's actual name. In one word, I assert that I Am not a fictional figment of anyone's imagination or a handy construct serving as a psychological crutch. I Am, and you'd better believe it. And remember, there's a whiff of timelessness about that conjugation, so not only Am I, but I Was and Shall Be. Beautiful! My Name also establishes that Who or What I Am is not reliant on any outside forces. I Am Going To Be Whoever I Am Going To Be, Mister, And There's Nothing You Or Anyone Else In The Universe Can Do About It. So in three simple words, both My existence (past, present and future) and the impervious nature of My sovereignty are conveyed. And the fact that it's all in there (and more) like that, and there's not a quick, simple explanation of it, is another part of the power of My Name. The fact that My Name is mysterious and cannot easily be pinned down is mighty fitting, don't you think? Again, I wouldn't be much of a God if there was no mystery about Me, and My Name articulates that mystery right from the get go.

But because of its first person conjugation, that version of My Name only works when I Am the One saying it. (You didn't think We were done with this part, did you?) So, for conversational usage purposes, I shift My Name to a third person conjugation for Moses (mostly in the same imperfect tense), but even that isn't straightforward. How could it be? We're talking about Me here! So it's a derivative of all the above that conveys My existence past, present and future with a strong "He Is!" flavor, and it's spelled (and transliterated from Hebrew into English) *YHVH*.

Okay, get a cup of coffee, friend. Since We're talking about My Name, We Are going to be diligent in running a few more rabbits down their holes here. Grammar nerds, rejoice! Everybody else, hang in there, because I promise there will be a point at the end other than just the sheer delight of the obsessively compulsive English majors.

Language is a big deal all the time. It gives you symbols in which to think and communicate. Obviously, We Are using language right now. And obviously, since the whole calamitous Babel babble debacle, there are more languages out there than frozen yogurt flavor and topping combinations. It's no surprise that there are a large number of alphabets out there. You're used to this one with its roots in Latin. If you've made it past Kindergarten, you know you've got 26 letters and 5 full time vowels with "y" as a switch-hitter. The Hebrew alphabet has 23 gorgeous letters in it, not one of them a vowel. Pick up a Hebrew newspaper, and you won't see a vowel in it, friend. If you're

Hebrew, you'll know which vowels go where. It sounds harder than it is. It's all what you're used to. See how easy it is to do it with this phrase:

ll th kngs hrss nd ll th kngs mn

If you need a hint, it's a lick from a nursery rhyme about a fellow shaped like an egg. So Hebrew's like that all the time, and has been from the very beginning. Thus, all the books in My Book that were written in Hebrew were written without vowels. Not a problem. If you know Hebrew. So My Name is written *YHVH* – no vowels.

Still not a problem. If you know Hebrew. Because, of course, there are vowels in My Name. It's not just a breathy, buzzy sound you make without opening your lips when you try to pronounce just those four consonants by themselves![29] But there is a problem after all. No human knows what the vowels are in My Name any longer – at least in the form I Am telling Moses to use in conversation (and eventually writing) with everybody, which is pretty much the only way it can be used.[30]

No one knows what vowels are supposed to be in My Name anymore because of a perfect-storm convergence of issues, all of which happen to begin in around 600 B.C. in the neighborhood of the Babylonian captivity. We'll talk about that in a good while, but for now, you just have to know that My people, to whom I Am going to be faithful and provide the land I promised Abraham, are not going to hold up their end of the covenant; I will be forced to send them into exile as a consequence. Too late for a spoiler alert, eh? I'm going to assume that if you've made it this far with Me, you know what exile is. As people are transplanted from their homeland where Hebrew is spoken, they must learn the language of their new country in order to function and survive. While some of those in exile are eventually allowed to return to their land, the Romans eventually raze Jerusalem in 70 A.D., destroying the temple; then Emperor Hadrian finishes it off in 135, bringing an end to the Jewish state entirely. Talk about a spoiler alert.

And over generations of living dispersed among other nations, this Diaspora of Abraham's offspring uses the language of the Scriptures less and less. Of all things, though, language is probably at the top of the "use it or lose

---

[29] Loving that most of you just tried it though.
[30] Remember, while My Name is based on a third person imperfect of "to be," it's not exactly the same (that would be *YHYH*). I just *had* to make it My own.

it" list. Fortunately, a pocket of Hebrew scribes on the western shore of the Sea of Galilee wake up and smell the parchment in around 600 A.D. and realize that there are precious few people left who could pick up a scroll of Exodus and know what vowels to put where when they read it. These precious scholars, known as the Masoretes (from the Hebrew word for "tradition"), come up with a genius system of vowels that can be inserted into the already-written text in the piles of scrolls that contain Our sacred writings. It's essentially a system of dashes and dots (called "nekudot" from Hebrew for "dotting") that go above, below, and inside the Hebrew consonant characters.

Here's a quick before and after sample. This is the Hebrew text of "In the beginning, God created the heavens and the earth":

בראשית ברא אלהים את השמים ואת הארץ

And here it is with the vowels:

בְּרֵאשִׁית בָּרָא אֱלֹהִים אֵת הַשָּׁמַיִם וְאֵת הָאָרֶץ

Pretty ingenious system, right? No need to rewrite all your scrolls, just carefully insert your dots and dashes, and voilà, all the generations to come have a record of the vowels.

So why doesn't anybody know how to say My Name because they don't know the vowels?

The second front of the perfect storm I mentioned begins during the Babylonian exile as well. At that time, a tradition begins to take shape regarding My Name. The Hebrews are feeling the consequential punishment for their lack of holiness, and as a result, are focusing on how holy I Am. Which is good, because I. Am. Holy. We just established that again with Moses taking off his footwear and will continue to do so in various ways once We pick up the story line again here in a bit. First, let's finish this Name business and the tradition that develops in Babylon. The people in exile decide that since I Am holy (yes, I Am), and that My Name is therefore holy (yes, it is), then it would be best to never say it out loud.

If you're thinking, "Huh?" at this point, so Am I. Yes, I Am going to eventually emphasize My holiness to Moses, et al. by commanding that My Name not be used in anything but in proper and respectful interchange, but at no point Am I going to command that it not be used. These "Don't Say His Name" folks mean well, but they're taking what turns out to be a very serious matter into their own hands, and the repercussions of this *superstition* reach right into your life, friend. This "Unutterable Name" nonsense seems like such a great idea to everyone and becomes so ensconced in everyone's thinking, that within *three short centuries*, the human-made tradition of never saying My Name aloud is observed more than any of My Me-made ten commandments, or any other thing I actually *want* people to do (or not do, as required by the circumstance)!

So, by the time the Masoretic scribes are putting in their dot and dash vowels on the ancient scrolls of Scripture up there in Tiberias, it's been nearly a *millennium* since anyone spoke My Name aloud. Every time My Name – *YHVH* – comes along in the Scriptures, they've substituted something else (to which you may count on Our getting in a moment). So when it comes time to put the vowels in for My Name, NO ONE KNOWS WHAT THEY ARE ANYMORE!!! They've been lost to oblivion because of a well-meaning yet misguided superstition that, instead of honoring Me, has in fact wiped from human memory the sound of the sweetest Word a person could ever speak. If it sounds like I Am a little upset about this, then We Are all on the same page.

Let's unpack this a bit more. In terms of life lessons, this is as good a time as any for Me to warn you about traditions. They're fine with Me. As long as you keep them at a "traditional" level: things you develop that add meaning to your life in family or community, from mundane matters like what kind of cranberries you serve at Thanksgiving to weightier issues like the style of music or prayer you use in your worship of Me. Diversity is a key indicator of the vastness of My imagination and the depth of My love for you, friend. So go on and build those thoughtful traditions that speak to your heart. However, once these practices cross the line into being somehow *required* in order to be in right standing with Me or your community, then you've gone too far with them; and in doing so, even if you've got good intentions, you're going to mess something important up every time. This is especially true if your well-intentioned tradition conflicts with something I have said, or puts words in My mouth that I haven't said. Then you've *really* crossed the line.

Case in point: I never told anyone to never say My Name. If I didn't want people to say it, I wouldn't have told it to Moses, or anybody else for that matter. And here comes the big point of this whole discussion about My Name. Who knows your name? Okay, in your habitat of social networks and online databases,[31] pretty much everyone knows your name. But, what do people call you? (I realize as We step into this issue, that your response will depend very much on your age and resultant habitat.) Even you youngsters

---

[31] *Some* of you even remember phone books.

can get this concept, though. In habitats that still cling to a modicum of courtesy, how one addresses others, in terms of how they are named, is an indicator of level of relationship and respect. Strangers, superiors, and others in the relational distance are generally addressed with a respectful title along with their surname (a/k/a family name), such as Mr. Smith, Ms. Jones, Mrs. Finch or Miss Washington. In a few instances, their function within the community usurps these gender-specific prefixes with professional titles, such as President Kennedy, Reverend King, or Doctor Ramoray.

In habitats where some semblance of relational structure remains, a person's first name is only used with permission, a permission that is generally granted in the case of a closer, more intimate relationship. Families and friends are on a first-name basis. Try calling your grammar school principal by her first name, though, and she'll make sure you never say the word "Harriet" again!

Names are identity. Telling someone to call you by your first name can have significant meaning. Entrusting someone with a special "first name basis" level of access has lost a good deal of its importance, but you can still grasp what I Am getting at. Had you known President John F. Kennedy, think of how much your relationship with him would have shifted had he invited you to call him "Jack," or how your relationship with your doctor would shift if he said, "Don't call me Dr. Ramoray. Call me Drake."

That relational shift – that intimate access with someone in a station of life (exponentially) higher than yours – is what We Are getting at here. I give Moses My Name so that people will use it. So people – you, friend – will be on a first name basis with Me, the Creator of all things. I Am not threatened or made less holy by your using My Name. I'm not less God because you call Me "Yahveh." John F. Kennedy was still the President of those who called him "Jack." I'm still the God of those who call Me by My Name.

You caught that, didn't you? Hate to burst more of your Bible school bubbles, but My Name is not "Yahweh."[32] That's along the lines of calling President Kennedy "Jass" instead of "Jack." You see, there are no "W" sounds in Hebrew. The entire English-speaking world has fallen victim to what one could call the Volkswagen Effect.

If you aren't acquainted with the mellifluous sounds of the German language, you need to know that they use pretty much the same alphabet as yours with the exception of a couple dots of their own thrown in to make

---

[32] And here you thought I'd misspelled My own Name a couple times previously.

some of their vowels über-special on occasion. We're not worried about vowels in this case, though.

The sneaky thing about your similar alphabets is that the two languages (still talking about just German and English here – other languages are going to have to wait for your own editions) your alphabets associate different phonetic sounds with the same characters. In the case of the word "Volkswagen" (nouns are capitalized in German all the time, another fun feature), the "V," which is pronounced in English with the same sound as that in "very vocal vampires," has instead an "F" sound in German, as in "famous freakish frogs." So German's "Volks" is pronounced "folks" in English. The German language **does** have the same "V" sound as English, but they use a "W" for it.[33]

"W" in German stands for "V" in English. Got it? Berliners say "Vagen", not "wagon". They have "Vieners" not "wieners."[34] So why Am I picking on them already? Well, the folks that brought you fahrvergnügen have also had some very deep thinkers over the years: Einstein, Goethe, Kant, Nietzsche, etc…, and a monk named Martin Luther. There is much We could look at in him and his time, but for these purposes We will simply note that a major step taken by Luther is the translation of The Owner's Manual into a language other than Latin (into which it had been translated by a scholar named Jerome a good thousand years earlier). Thus, German is the first vernacular language[35] into which TOM gets translated. In examination of the text, Luther and further German scholars transliterate My Name from Hebrew, "יהוה,"[36] into "JHWH" because the "W" is their "V" sound (and the "J" is their "Y" sound – hang in there!).

The Masoretic Hebrew vowel dots actually put My Name out as "Yehvah,"[37] but it sounds much stronger to start My Name with "Yes!" ("Jah"

---

[33] This, inexplicably, seems to be the root of Mr. Chekhov's very un-Russian accent, yielding "wery wocal wampires" in spite of the prolific abundance of "V" sounds in his supposedly native tongue. But We digress.

[34] Actually, a "Wiener" in German is a man from Wien – Vienna – and what you call a wiener is what they call a sausage, "Wurst" (pronounced "Vurst", remember), and their Wurst is the best!

[35] Latin may have fallen into this category for a handful of locals, but it was more fully the language of the Roman Empire. The language of each person's heart is usually the one their mother sang to them in, not the Empire's. Cue the Imperial March if you know it.

[36] Remember to read that right to left, now.

[37] Still a guess on the Masoretes' part. As such, We'll stick with Yahveh since it's just as likely and requires only one edit on what you're accustomed to instead of two.

in German), so I'm "Yahweh" in the mountains of German scholarship to follow in passionate study of and writing about TOM, each German scholar hearing a "v" sound at the sight of each "w," the "w" which will simply be copied into this and other languages with a somewhat casual regard to phonetics. Thus, at the end of this whole swirl of linguistic factors, it probably comes as a surprise that I Am actually Yahveh in English. If you can't manage that, I'll answer to "Yahweh" too. I can handle it. But since We Are on a first name basis and all, I thought you should know all this.

Okay, just one more rabbit to run down its hole here and We'll be back on the mountain with Moses. Let's return your thoughts to the time when this tradition of not speaking My Name aloud began. This ancient time is a habitat in which literacy is a luxury. So are books, which are not yet in the codex form that line your shelves. (Want to know what a codex is? Look at a book – papers stacked on top of each other and bound on one side. You may be holding one.) For millennia, writing was instead found in stone or clay, but mostly in scrolls made of either animal skin or papyrus, all of which were written by hand, making them rare and costly. Not something everyone has in their home to ponder over whenever they like, if they are even literate.

The scrolls containing The Owner's Manual are invested in and owned by the community, and read aloud and studied and discussed in community. Far more people take My Words in through their ears in hearing them read aloud than take them in through their eyes. In other words, there's a whole lot of reading out loud going on. So if you're the one reading aloud a passage of Scripture and come across My Name, "יהוה/*YHVH*," but are not supposed to say it, what are you going to do? Point to the sky with a shrug of your shoulders? Say "You Know Who" or "The Big Guy Upstairs?" Well, of course not, especially since the genesis of this tradition lies in a lopsided interpretation of My holiness.

No, the tradition develops that, instead of using My perfectly fine and usable name – the name that was good enough for Moses to use and declare aloud, good enough for David and Samson and Esther and Ruth and Solomon and every other prophet or writer! No, instead of My Name, the word "LORD," *"ADONAI"*[38] in Hebrew, is spoken anytime My Name appears in the text. Very respectful, but very much not what I Was hoping for when I put Us on a first name basis with humans.

---

[38] Hebrew has neither lowercase nor uppercase letters, though many will say it's all uppercase. I'm not shouting at you. Yet.

Drumroll, please. That *is* what this whole tirade is all about: relation-ship, and more particularly, the level of distance forced into Our relationship with you by this superstitious tradition. And you may be thinking you're far removed from this whole thing, but you're not, friend. In the original Hebrew text of The Owner's Manual, My Name is there in print close to 7,000 times. If it were going to be translated/transliterated into English, then "Yahweh," "Yahveh," "Yehvah," or something like them would be there in your copy the same number of times, but it's not. My Name is not printed in your Bible. MY NAME IS NOT PRINTED IN MY BOOK! (If I had ears, steam would be coming out of them right now.) No, the same tradition that started in 600 B.C. Babylon still holds sway in your habitat, friend: Instead of My powerful, beautiful, relational-access-laden Name, your Bible has "LORD" printed in every instance My Name appears in the original text.[39] In the instances where the Hebrew text actually says *"ADONAI"* (again, Hebrew for "Lord"), it's written with regular characters, "Lord."[40] The fact that My Name substitute, "LORD,"[41] has small caps is the indicator that MY NAME IS SUPPOSED TO BE THERE INSTEAD.[42]

So all those texts you tried to memorize as a kid? You learned them wrong along with the rest of humanity over the last two millennia. Take Deuteronomy 6:4, "The LORD our God, the LORD is one." That's "Yahweh our God, Yahweh is one." Or the next sentence, "You shall love the LORD your God with all your heart and with all your soul and with all your might." That should read "You shall love Yahweh your God with all your heart..." Yes, I'm your Lord, I Am THE Lord, as I was in the beginning and ever shall be, world without a thank you very much. But you've been on a first Name basis with Me and not known it, friend. Let that sink deeper into your soul every time you see "LORD".[43]

---

[39] Unless you're one of the perspicacious handful of enthusiasts that have a Names of God Bible or the World English Bible. (Feel free to interpret this statement as a recommending endorsement.)

[40] As in Exodus 4:10, for example.

[41] To see an example in your own Bible, scan nearly any page and you'll come up with plenty. It's like shooting fish in a barrel. Believe Me, We Are not going to let you forget any of this.

[42] Yes, I AM SHOUTING THIS.

[43] This tradition is universal. Remember when Luther translated The Owner's Manual into German? That 1545 edition maintains the same Don't Say the Name tradition, and I Am referred to as "der HERR," in close equivalent to the "LORD" in your translations. Newer German translations shift to your sporty small caps with "der HERR."

This entire *ADONAI* substitution practice, by the way, is where the whole "Jehovah" misfire comes from. That little tradition popped up several hundred years ago when, faced with the same predicament of knowing the vowels of My Name had been lost, some well-meaning genius arbitrarily fused the known consonants of My Name with the known vowels in an entirely different word: *ADONAI*. Yes, it's the Hebrew word for "Lord," which, again, I Am, as in My role and station, but it's not My Name. And so We burst another Bible bubble, particularly for you fans of the King James Version, though it only sports "Jehovah" seven times. I will give these folks a good deal of credit, though, for getting the "v" sound right, and particularly for at least making the attempt at getting My Name out of the mothballs. I've never quite gotten the logic, though. I mean, it's clear that the vowels of an entirely different word are used with My Name consonants, but that seems more like a parlor game than anything else. Like renaming your guest Frederick "Fradeyrack" for the night because he's a car salesman.

As for Me and "Jehovah," all you've got to do is take out that extra "o" forced by the *YHVH/ADONAI* mashup, and you're in business with as close to the real deal as you can get for now. Okay. Thanks for letting Me get that off My anthropomorphized chest. I feel much better now knowing that you know all that. Now, where were We? That's right: on the mountain with Basketboy in Our very first chat with him.

Chapter 10

Mountain to Mountain

So here We Are on the mountain, Moses and Me, and We've finished Our introductions and Are on a first-Name basis with all the resonance implied therein. Now the fun starts. I commission Moses with two missions: first, to gather the elders of Israel together and let them in on Our plans; then, to go with those elders to the king and "negotiate" with Pharaoh for the release of My people.[1]

The elders, of course, are the easier of those two tasks, but even they may need convincing, and Moses says so. Who can blame him after his quick but checkered past with his Hebrew brethren? Therefore, in order to back up the testimony Moses will share with them of speaking with Me directly, I provide him with the ability to perform a few signs.[2] These will be things that point to My power and presence with him. (This also is setting a precedent for the future: When I very much want someone's message to be heard, I will perform signs through them in order to credibly establish that their words are from Me.) Of course you know about Moses' staff: When he throws it on the ground, it'll turn into a snake. Since not many of you live in snaky habitats any longer, the import of My telling Moses to then pick it up by its tail may be lost on you. Grab a snake by the tail, get a snake bite. Not Moses, though. He grabs a snake by the tail, it turns into his famous staff. Do not try this at home.

The other signs with which I equip Moses in order to establish his credibility are often lost. The second is on the creepy side and definitely not as sexy as hail that starts fires, so it doesn't make it into your movies. I have Moses put his hand inside the fold of his robe above his belt; when he pulls it

---

[1] Exodus 3:16–18, and following. All cites in this chapter are in Exodus unless otherwise noted.
[2] Exodus 4:1–8.

out, his hand is covered with the white flakes of leprosy. Yep. When he puts it back into his robe, it comes out clean and restored. (You can see how that feature gets passed over in Hollywood.) The third sign gets balled up with a later plague: Moses is to take some water from the Nile and pour it on the ground, where it becomes blood (not exactly how the plague plays).

These may seem like minor magic tricks in comparison with what you know is coming, but keep context in mind and recall that this is the very beginning of Our altering natural order in some way to indicate Our powerful presence. We have, of course, done a bit of this already, but have restricted Ourselves largely to the facilitation of conception in the barren – not something that takes place before your very eyes as the transformation of Moses' staff, hand, and river water will.

However, even equipped with these signs, Moses is more than hesitant, and comes up with his next excuse. The first one – that nobody's going to believe him – is logical, hence the signs. This next one makes sense too, and the poor fellow has been bad-mouthed about it for many years. Over the years, people in your habitat have blasted as a lame excuse Moses' protest about not being able to speak well, as something along the lines of most people's distaste for speaking in public. It's more than that for him, though. You see, Moses literally is "bad mouthed."[3] He stutters. That's right. Makes perfect sense on a psychological level, doesn't it? As a double-identity child growing up with an unstable sense of self, not having a deeply grounded sense of being Hebrew or Egyptian? Having that hesitance of spirit manifest in uneasy speech?

Know why you haven't heard about it? Two reasons. First: Me. I'll eventually make everyone forget that Moses ever had a problem with his speaking, because I *will* fix his mouth and he'll have so much to say they'll be tired of hearing him. We've got Ourselves a built-in sign here, friends. And I say as much to Moses. "Who do you think made that mouth of yours, boy? If I can turn a stick into a snake, I can free your tongue and lips to work right." But at this point, that hesitancy is deep in his psyche, and even after My promise to smooth out his speech, he still persists in trying to get out of the job, asking Me to send somebody else.

Which really steams Me. Still does. When I clearly set someone to do something like I Am doing here with Moses, and all they can come up

---

[3]   Which gets translated "slow of speech and tongue" in most versions of Exodus 4:10–12. The Hebrew for "slow" there has a feel of dragging heaviness to it. Hence, Our next sentence.

with are reasons why it can't happen, I have to play the Who Do You Think You're Talking To card. Back to the bush here. The bush is not making the flame. I Am. I'm the One Who's going to liberate Israel, not Moses. I'm the One Who's going to fight your battles, not you. I Am NEVER going to ask ANYONE to do something unless I Am prepared to see them through it. Unfortunately, My conversation with Moses happens long before Rogers and Hammerstein pen "You'll Never Walk Alone," and Moses is wrestling with some game-changing concepts in a time that is still way before anyone will be able to wrap their minds around My whole omnipresenceness (which should make it a whole lot easier for you to sense My nearness, by the way). So, I cut Basketboy some slack, and cave in and give Moses a partner on his mission: his brother, Aaron, the other reason you don't know about Moses' stutter. Aaron is actually perfectly situated as a Hebrew elder himself now, which will help Moses' credibility with them, and will help the humble shepherd feel like he's not alone. I could have done it all without Aaron in the picture, but as a gift to Moses, I bring his older brother (by three years) onto the delivery team. Call it grace, unmerited favor. Look around and you'll find it all over your life too.

Well, Our allowing Aaron to come along for the adventure clinches it for Moses, and he's finally all in. Remember, I wasn't going to force him on this mission, any more than I'm going to force you to follow Us On The Way. He chooses to accept his assignment, and We're off to the races. Or at least to Egypt.

So Moses brings Aaron up to speed on everything, and they go before the elders of the Hebrews and give them the news that the game's afoot. Aaron is a full partner with Moses in this, even performing the three signs I'd given Moses as convincing proofs of My working through him. When the Hebrew elders hear The Plan and see the proofs, you know what they do first? Is their first considered act to select a team of their strongest to storm the palace? Do they immediately tell the people what they've just heard? Start planning the best exit route? Nope, none of those. They put first things first and bow down and worship Me.[4] The most momentous of moments for these folks in over four hundred years, and look what they do! It still brings tears to My anthropomorphic eyes. Take a lesson, friend, and mark the seams in your life in My presence. Going into something major? Worship Me. Coming out of something major? Worship Me. You get the point.

---

4 Exodus 4:27–31.

What happens next borders on the anticlimactic. I've heard the Hebrews' cries, I've cajoled and commissioned Moses, brought his brother in at his request, broken the news to the elders, and done all the necessary buildup. So, everything has been leading up to the very next moment, a crescendo of destiny wherein all of history turns on the next climactic conversation.

Only it doesn't. No massive demonstration. No march on the palace gates. Just two brothers who get an audience with Pharaoh, who's back in the story.[5] (Actually, this is the son of the kinglet who was around when Moses left Egypt. Remember, 40 years have passed.) Their conversation has none of the drama or signs, and feels almost like a prelude. This, of course, is because you know what's coming. Try to pretend you don't for a minute. Pharaoh sure doesn't. All he knows is that he's got two Hebrews before him. (Though Pharaoh would have known him, Moses wouldn't have even amounted to half-breed status in the king's eyes.) The Hebrews are telling him that their God, Yahveh, has told them to ask him – the most powerful (human) king of his time – to give the entire workforce a vacation.

Now, if you haven't yet, I really do need you to bust out your Manual and read even just the first three verses of Exodus' fifth chapter. With your newly-gained knowledge about My name, make sure you insert "Yahveh" for LORD all four times and see if it changes things a bit.

Then, notice that the opening request We make of Pharaoh is that he let the Hebrews take a journey for three days into the wilderness and there hold a festival of sacrifice in worship of Me. Implied in this request is that they'll come back when they're done. No need to go down the road of "What if Pharaoh had let them go? Would they have had to come back?" He didn't. They didn't. Just wanted to point out that there was a pretty rosy option there at the beginning for Baldy, but he didn't take it. There's a thumbnail lesson in there for you, friend: Obey early and things'll work out exponentially better for you. But, let Us keep moving.

Now, as We drew your attention to a moment ago, when Moses and Aaron convey My message, they use My Name. They don't say, "This is what the Lord, the God of Israel says." They say, "This is what *Yahveh*, the God of Israel says." At this point, neither I nor they are asserting any kind of monotheism. The substitution of "*the* LORD" in the text implies so, however. Though We Are on that journey, it's far from time to make those kinds of

---

[5]   As We cross into Exodus 5, this is an excellent time to read the fast-moving account of all that follows in TOM.

assertions. We Are not necessarily even asserting supremacy over other "gods" at this point – another implication of the substitution of "LORD" for My name in the text. We Are still relating to people where they're at – both the Hebrews *and* the Egyptians. They're all still very localized in their thinking both in terms of My having a physical location (out in the wilderness) along with the implied assumption that other locations harbor other deities. That's certainly Pharaoh's frame of reference. He knows Ra, Thoth, and several other gods that have their own specific territories or responsibilities in Egypt, but I'm not on his radar yet. "Who's this Yahveh that I should listen to him and let Israel go? Never heard of him!"

Remember, Moses has "only" asked him for a religious holiday at this point, one that Israel at least theoretically is going to come back from. Any good manager knows that time off refreshes workers, builds loyalty, and yields better results when employees return to work. Pharaoh has no MBA, though, and can only see that there are Hebrews chatting with him now that should be out there building something (not just the brothers, actually, but the Hebrew elders who've come along to represent their people). In the king's mind, if the slaves have got time for vacation, they've got too much time on their hands. In that case, they've got time to gather their own straw to make all the bricks required for the construction projects.

Now, you've seen these structures. The Hebrew slaves are putting thousands of bricks a day into them. And Pharaoh thinks that, since they apparently have this surplus time, they can use that to get their straw (freeing the straw-gatherers for other work, you'd suppose) and still have enough time to make the same number of bricks as usual. Pharaoh thinks himself very clever to come up with this form of punishment for such an outlandish demand.

Note that word, "demand." As in, I did not ask puny Pharaoh, "Would you please be so kind as to give My people a few days off?" That's the kind of language he's accustomed to. So the way I treat him is at best as a peer, if not as a subordinate. I speak to him in the form of an imperative (a command, if you're not a grammar nerd), rather than a request: "Let My people go, that they may hold a Festival to Me in the wilderness."[6] This elicits an instant barrier in Pharaoh's heart. His pride erects a hard, thick wall against Me, for how dare anyone speak to Pharaoh in the tone of command as I have done through Moses? Baldy fancies himself the greatest force in the universe, and

---

[6] Exodus 5:1.

any request made of him had better be in the grovel position with a big "pretty please" on top. Right.

Pharaoh's also a savvy slave-driver. He knows this Get Your Own Straw tactic will turn the Hebrews against Moses in two ways. In fact, Pharaoh says himself[7] that having to work this much harder will keep them from listening to Moses. For one thing, they're going to have to work even longer hours to get their quota of bricks made, so there won't be time at the end of the day to throw together any revolt rallies. For another, Pharaoh is rightly betting that the slaves will blame Moses for this extra work, driving a wedge between his construction workers and their organizing union-boss-wanna-be. So far, this is all about work to Baldy. (Watch him as We go through the upcoming drama with him. He's going to act more like he's dealing with a labor union than with a God.)

The straw tactic does just what Pharaoh expects: It turns the Hebrews[8] against Moses, which turns Moses against Me, "I thought You sent me to deliver these people, not make life worse for them! Exactly when is this whole rescue part going to kick in?" This is understandable, but Moses fails to see this opening exchange for what it is: Even to Pharaoh, the oppressor of My people, I extend the grace of the option to do the right thing, to make the right choice to free the Hebrews without experiencing any consequence from having enslaved them. That's a decided part of Who I Am: Everybody gets a chance at some point. This is Pharaoh's. He still thinks *he's* the power king in the equation, though, and misses his opportunity to get out of the whole mess without so much as a skinned sphinx as a result.

Okay, I realize I've already said a couple times that We Are on the brink of destiny here, but now We *really* Are. And now I *really* want you to read My answer to Moses' questions because it pretty much sums up where We've been, and where and why We're going: an excellent perspective-setter. So bust out, or rather, would you please be so kind as to bust out your Owner's Manual again online or on lap and slowly read Exodus 6:1–8?[9] Ready? Go!

Lots of important things in here. They set up what to look for in the coming drama. Chief among the themes are "My mighty hand." As We've been pointing out from the beginning, at crucial junctures of Our shepherding

---

[7] Exodus 5:9.

[8] Exodus 5:20–21.

[9] Do feel free to take in the preceding context too if you've not done that yet. Oh, and one last reminder: Once again, every time your text says "the LORD," it really says *YHVH*, or in your closest pronunciation for the time being, "Yahveh," My Name. Yes, clearly, it matters to Me.

humanity, things are moved forward in ways that point directly to Me/My power as the primary moving force. This happens in each of the first three generations of The Abraplan with Abraham, Isaac, and Jacob. This is why My name is linked with theirs so often: a reminder of My power establishing and moving The Plan forward in each of their lives.

I've made it clear that Moses is part of the Abraplan too. What I make clear in the passage you should have just read (here's a second chance for you slackers) is that in some ways I Am taking Moses to a higher level even than old Abraham himself. In fact I already have. In case you thought I was over-focused on a first-Name-basis fixation before, verse 3 should have changed your mind. Neither Abraham, Isaac, nor Jacob knew My Name; they knew Me only as *EL-SHADDAI*, God of the Mountain.[10] Remember, I Am working long term here, and with "*EL-SHADDAI*" and its associations working deep in their psyche about Me, when the Hebrews finally get to Sinai, they'll be all, "Oh, *this* is His mountain!" Thus, when Moses comes down from "My" mountain with The Big Ten and Other Instructions, every-one will be certain it's all come from Me. Which will be a good thing.

These verses in Exodus 6 should also solidify your sense of My keeping My promises. I know the Hebrews feel forgotten. The Abraplan has been moving forward this whole time, but because of their limited perspective within small periods of time, My people have not been able to see anything but their instant situation. I have seen the whole saga the whole time, and through it all have had in mind the end to which all things are moving. They have served their time in this unpleasant but necessary chapter, and I Am about to free them – both to relieve them of their bondage, and to also keep My covenant promises. Those covenant promises, you'll recall, are not sim-ply about the offspring of Abraham, now poised for deliverance, but concern ultimately the deliverance of all humanity – including you – when The Time comes. So if you're trapped in an unpleasant chapter, hang in there, kid. The Time will come. We will complete the Abraplan.

In the meantime, let Us briefly underscore something about emotion, specifically that of discouragement being felt by the Hebrews (and maybe even you) right now, which is linked to timing. We just processed timing, now let's look at feelings. I Am not faulting My children for feeling this way;

---

[10] That mellifluous moniker has taken on more meaning since ("Almighty," generally, as in your translation here) because of its association with Me. However, the word's initial roots are in the mountain, so to speak. Neither Abraham nor Moses heard "Almighty" in *SHADDAI*. They heard "mountain."

given their perspective, it'd be impossible to *not* feel discouraged. What I want to point out here, as I will elsewhere On The Way, is that My action is not dependent on how humans feel. Right now, Our people feel like We have forgotten them, that their trust in Moses was ill-placed, and that they're sinking into misery even deeper than before. They feel like I have abandoned them. However, their simply feeling those things does not make them true. In fact, the truth is the opposite of what they're feeling: I have not forgotten them, Moses is going to pull through with flying colors, and they're going to be launched out of their misery into freedom.

The bottom line of this excursion? Feeling something doesn't make it true. Though you may feel like it, I promise you that I have neither forgotten nor abandoned you. And I want you to take heart in knowing that, in spite of how you may feel right now, I Am still at work, albeit behind the scenes for a longer time than you'd like. I can and will intervene in the Hebrews' lives here in a moment, and that action is coming because it is the right time for it. I do not have to wait until My children feel hopeful, cheerful, joyful or any other –ful associated with a sappy greeting card. I can and will intervene in your life at just the right time as well, and that action will be driven not by how you feel about Me, but by how I feel about you. And you are more precious and priceless to Me than the limited range of human vocabulary can describe.

So the next step in the Abraplan is to get this supernaturally-fertile-now-bodaciously-numerous[11] nation of Israel out of Egypt and into their own country. Abraham, Isaac and Jacob had lived in the land of Canaan, but as tented visitors. Now, though, their descendants will be putting their tents away and living in permanent homes. Well, maybe not now, but soon. Well, relatively soon. They've got to get there first. So, as you can see, I remind Moses of the whole big picture, and affirm that I Am going to stretch out My hand in mighty acts of wonder and judgment to fulfill My promises. When He relays My noble speech to the Hebrews, though, they're too discouraged from their harsh situation to notice. Which is okay. I'm about to give everybody a few things to notice here.

The time has finally come to take the gloves off. I tell Moses to go back to Pharaoh. Moses sees no reason to think things are going to be any different. The Israelites, the ones who are supposedly on Our side, won't believe him when he relays My words; how in the heck is Pharaoh going to listen? And he

---

[11] Pharaoh just remarked again about how many Hebrews there are in Exodus 5:5.

brings up the whole stuttering thing again, like I haven't already cleared Aaron for special agent service; but We go through it again. Moses, you get the Word from Me, then Aaron will get the Word from you. Aaron delivers My Word to Pharaoh. This time, if Baldy says, "No" again, do the snake thing.[12]

Now, We Are heading into some murky territory here, because the Egyptians are symbol people. Everything is or has a symbol. Yes, every language is symbolic, but their hieroglyphics are literally so. In addition, in their habitat, certain animals and bugs are symbols of this or that supposed god, who's a symbol of this or that department or territory of land or life, and so on. Well, the symbols are about to hit the fan, and they start with the snake. The Egyptians have this supernatural supersnake in their mythology called Apep, who among other things supposedly has the ability to swallow the sun. So when Pharaoh turns a deaf ear to Moses and Aaron, Aaron throws down the staff just as I instructed, and just as I promised, it turns into a snake. Well, the Egyptian sorcerers who dabble in the dark side are able to do the same with their staffs; only My snake gobbles theirs up. Swallows them whole. With the story of Apep and his threat to gobble the sun in their minds, the Egyptians see an opening summary of how My power is going to dominate and consume what little efforts they can muster against Us. Of course, it's going to take more than this snake snack to move proud Pharaoh.

Thus, the wonders We have promised fall upon Egypt in order to break the pride of Pharaoh. That's right. The plagues. Each one shows My sovereign rule over some area of life over which the Egyptians have at least one of their many "gods"[13] presiding. I limit Myself to ten plagues, because if I were to hit each of the "gods" on Egypt's menu at the time, there'd have been nothing left of them; you see, My mercy is hidden everywhere, even (and often, especially) in My judgment. I could wipe Egypt out completely – that would certainly free the Hebrews – but I don't. I act like a parent even to the slave-driving nation and render a consequence every time Pharaoh disobeys Me. It takes him ten times to finally obey; besides, ten carries the weight and sense of fullness and completeness.[14] So as long as We Are going to fully step into symbols here, let Us do a decent job of it.

---

[12] Exodus 6:9–12; 6:28–7:9.

[13] Pardon Our repeated use of quotation marks around the term "god" or "gods," but it seems less ponderous than writing "supposed gods" or "alleged gods" every time. Simply not capitalizing the word isn't quite enough in Our book in terms of making clear their lack of existence.

[14] Gee, what other set of ten is on the horizon?

You can skim the next several chapters (commencing in Exodus 7:14) of your Owner's Manual and check all the headings for the list of what's to come: blood, frogs, gnats, flies, stricken livestock, boils, hail, locusts, darkness, and stricken firstborn. It might not look like it at first blush, but there's a crescendo built into that sequence as things get more and more serious, powerful, and wider in impact as We go along. And as I said, each escalating plague is a direct incursion into the territory of one or more Egyptian "gods" who, if they exist, should show up to the party and in the very least make for an interesting duel before I whup their sorry deific behinds. Of course, each Egyptian deity is a no show.

Speaking of no show, you'll also note that their "gods" have received the same treatment as Pharaoh: They are nameless in Our account. Their names are insignificant because they are insignificant. Well, something has to actually exist before it can be insignificant, so Pharaoh is insignificant; his gods are nonexistent. If you really want to geek out on the whole sequence, though, plenty of your scholars have spent the time lining up which plague is targeted at which alleged god. Now's not the time to get distracted by a bunch of Egyptology, though. That's why they're not mentioned in the story: It's not about them, it's about Me. And honestly, it's more about Pharaoh than his "gods" in terms of who's being shown to be impotent in these plagues.

But to keep you here instead of having you bounce off to Wikipedia or elsewhere, here's a quick, and I mean quick, summary. A few of these fall in territories covered by more than one Egyptian "god," but We won't take time for the whole panoply here. Let's just note the main culprits. Plague one: Bloody Nile (as well as streams, canals, ponds, buckets, jars) is a direct attack on Hapi, Egypt's supposed god of the Nile. Life requires water as well as blood, obviously in different functions. I Am the Source of all life and can shift creation as I please, a common theme throughout these ten episodes.

Next come the frogs, and I mean everywhere. Under the pillows and down in the cookie jars. This comes against Heket, their frog-headed "goddess" of fertility, another area over which I've already well established My sovereignty. Remember how I've been building the Hebrews into a swarm? Swarming bugs and reptiles is a piece of cake after swarming humans all these years.

After the frogs come the gnats, and this plague has a special feature that makes it one of My favorites. You see, the frogs and other creatures that descend on Baldy and his crew are all already alive when this showdown starts. I just corral them all into ultra-high density when the time comes. Not so the gnats. I create them out of the dust of Egypt. Every speck of Egyptian dust becomes a gnat at My command. Now *that's* a lot of gnats. So they're everywhere, bugging (!) every human or animal in Egypt – hair, nose, eyes, ears, mouth. A lot of extra protein that day in the form of gnats getting eaten or inhaled. And once again, Geb – their purported god of earth and ground (and dust), whose laughs are supposed to cause earthquakes – does not show up to keep Me from creating life with "his" dust. Nor does Amun, kind of their big daddy god who's supposed to be able to do this sort of thing himself. Turns out, just as in Eden, I Am the only One who can create life from dust. Or anything else, for that matter.

Which by now is pretty clear, even to major players on the other team. In the spirit of full disclosure here, I should mention that, as they did with the staff/snake thing, Pharaoh's dark sorcerers are able to pony up the necessary mojo to mimic the first two plagues – that would be changing water to blood, and summoning an army of frogs. However, that's where their efforts peter out. They take one look at the gnats I make from dust and turn in their wands, telling Pharaoh that, "This is the finger of God!" Nothing else can explain it.[15] That, friend, is music to My ears (and a testimony you can still hear today from people whose eyes have been opened On The Way).

Okay, as long as We're breaking things down a bit, the plague of gnats ends the first set of three. We're establishing a pattern that's going to repeat itself, so We'll have three sets of three[16] with a final climax when We're through. We Are not going to do a blow by blow here – you can do that on your own, and I hope you have already. Each set, as in plagues one, four and seven, starts with a morning conversation with Baldy. Then the second of each set finds Me simply sending Moses to go to Pharaoh (with no time of day specified) with Our demand and warning, and for the third in each set, there's a bit of a three-strikes-and-you're-out dynamic.[17] Since Baldy's not responded to the previous two requests, he gets hit with a bonus third plague in each set without warning in an effort to ramp up his motivation to obey when We have Our next morning conversation with him.

One other little feature is that, after the first set of three in which Aaron does the talking to Pharaoh (and the hand or staff stretching that triggers the resultant plague), his brother handles those that remain. Moses himself

---

[15] Exodus 8:18–19.

[16] If you've not noticed yet, three is a favorite number of Ours.

[17] Of course Pharaoh didn't know baseball, but you do.

has been so convinced by the wonders that, "By golly, if Yahveh can do the blood, frog and gnat wonders, then my little speech impediment isn't going to get in His way."

With the Nile/blood and dust/gnat plagues, We establish that I Am the Lord of the water and earth; and so with the fourth plague of flies, I Am clearly in charge of the air – and what's in it – too. This steps right on the toes of the Egyptian "god" Shu, who's supposed to handle the air department, but can't shoo a single fly away.[18] Of course, the gnats were in the air too,[19] but it will also contain the hail and locusts, so everybody gets a share of the air, and it's all good. Shu doesn't show those times either.

These flying flies are everywhere, covering everything. Ever feel a fly bite? Head to the Adirondacks or the woodlands of northern Maine the end of May, and you'll get a sample of the Egyptians' experience. Ask anyone who's been in a swarm of black flies, and they'll tell you they'd have done *anything* to escape them. So it's no surprise that Pharaoh actually budges in the wake of the flyfestation. At first, he tries to have his cake and eat it too – Baldy tells Moses the Hebrews can have their sacrifice festival, but they have to do it within Egypt's borders. Moses doesn't budge, so Pharaoh gives in (for a moment) and tells them to go ahead and do it outside Egypt, but pretty much right over the border in order to be able to get them right back to work when they're done.[20]

This is going to be a pattern that repeats as the plagues get harsher. Pharaoh will acquiesce when directly facing the consequences to his people – as in when the upcoming plagues are actually underway. But when Moses brings the curtain down on the current plague, and the consequences are gone, so is Pharaoh's largesse. He changes his mind and doesn't let anyone go anywhere. Even when he's "giving in," though, Baldy still doesn't understand that he's not in a position to negotiate with Me. He tries to have the sacrifices done in-country. Another time, he'll ask Moses to leave the Hebrew women and children behind[21] to ensure the men's return. He still doesn't understand that I Am not some mortal neighbor king with whom to build a compromise. (Several in your habitat continue to suffer from this affliction in their regard of Me.)

---

[18] Yes, I can hear your groan, but I just had to!
[19] Their genesis in dust is their main feature.
[20] Exodus 8:25–32.
[21] Exodus 10:10–11.

Okay, where were We? Livestock are next. Pharaoh is warned that unless he lets My people go, all Egyptian animals out in the field will be toast. (Conversely, the Hebrews' animals will be fine as a frog's hair, just as they were when the flies came, etc.) Now, from here on, in this and future pestilential plagues, you've got a bit of a smorgasbord to choose from in the Egyptian deity menu in terms of whose territory We're proving Ourselves sovereign over. In terms of the field stock dropping in their tracks without a peep from Egypt's supposed guardian gods, you've got your dog-headed Anubis (judgment, life and death), and Hathor (protection). When the boils hit the Egyptian humans next, neither Isis nor her sister Nephtys (alleged to have healing powers along with a handful of other deities) show up to cure a one.

Seth, in charge of storms, doesn't stop the mother of all hail storms; neither does Nut, the goddess who's supposed to dictate sky usage. (By this stage of the game, half of Pharaoh's officials are betting on Me and make sure their people and what's left of their herds are well inside when they hear Moses predict this hail storm.) Hailstones the size of frozen Cornish game hens pummel the earth, destroying crops, stripping bark off trees, and nailing everything else that hasn't sought shelter. Spectacular lightning and deafening, tooth-crunching thunder too, of course, like any good hailstorm; except in Goshen, where My people look up and ask each other, "Did you hear something?"

Like before, Pharaoh says "Okay, I'll let you go, just stop the hail and the thunder," but after I reign them in, he withdraws his withdrawal approval. Enter, then, the classic Biblical plague: locusts. These critters are going to eat any plant still living after the flies and hail have already ravaged things. You've got territorial Egyptian deity choices here too: Senehem has a locust head himself, poor fellow, and is supposed to keep the flying eating machines away. His buddy, Osiris, does supposed double duty from the underworld and keeps an eye on crops too. Like Osiris is pushing produce up out of the ground from the underworld or something. Right. And in case you've not been noticing as We've gone along here, the supply of meat has been cut down to next to nothing between the field deaths and the hail, and what grain had survived the hail is now locust lunch. Pharaoh shouldn't be worrying about who's going to build his pyramids, but about who's going to feed his people.

Which triggers an associated flashback: Remember how My people got into Egypt in the first place. My placement of Joseph in that Egyptian prison so that by the gifts I gave him, that precious son of Jacob could save the entire region from starvation. The Pharaoh that trusted My voice in Joseph then was blessed with an abundance of grain to feed all in need. This Pharaoh that will not listen to My voice through Moses has brought a complete end to the cycle: The storehouses of blessing and of grain are shut tight.

Now, much is said about the Egyptian "god," Ra, king of their whole deific chessboard, in charge of the sun, and the patron deity of Pharaoh. So the final plague (of the three threes, that is) is a direct assault on both Pharaoh and his petty patron sun god: the plague of darkness. This one is totally Ra's party, and everybody knows it, but even though he's supposed to have the sun in his backseat, Egypt stays dark as day turns to unscheduled night. Actually, darker than night. You don't know this dark, friend, and I hope you never will. This is no eclipse with a rosy 360° sunset nor heavy cloud with a good bit of ambient light left. This is outside-at-noon-but-can't-see-my-own-hand-in-front-of-me dark that feels like it has a hold on you and isn't pushed away by the light of any fire or lamp. So when I say total darkness falls on Egypt, it feels somehow like there's a blanket of darkness weighing down on everyone, and it's more total than you can imagine. And it lasts for... (drumroll...) three days. Three days of not being able to move except by touch, even out in the middle of the street (thus, not much moving going on). It is so devastating that Pharaoh has another moment of conscience and says he'll release the Hebrews for a festival – as long as they leave their flocks and herds behind as collateral. When Moses replies that those will be needed for the sacrifice, it's still a no go from Pharaoh. [22]

Now, before We get to the big climax, let Us look back on what's happened so far. In three sets of three, We have told Pharaoh to temporarily release Our people so that they can worship Me in the wilderness. Each time, Pharaoh says no. When the consequences of the plagues ramp up, he says yes, but always with a condition first – do it here in Egypt, don't take your women, don't take your animals – so that he would "get something" out of the transaction and thus prove he is still the powerful king of Egypt, able to gain concessions from the desert god he supposes Me to be. The wall of pride in his heart has only grown stronger in the process, mortified that anyone – even a god – should make demands of him. However, as time has gone along, the officials of his court and the people of his land have turned their hearts against him, as they're the ones feeling most intensely the painful consequences from his refusal to give in to a clearly Higher Power. They're actually rooting for Moses at this stage of the game, not just

---

[22] The women and children were allowed to go this time (Exodus 10:24–27).

to prevent further plagues on themselves, but because they've actually taken his side[23] – Our side, the side of the Hebrews – in the matter.

You see, the Egyptian people have gotten the whole point of the lesson. They've seen with their own eyes (and felt on their own property and skin) the proof of My existence in the wonders I have done in their midst. They know that I Am, and they also know that, in the very least, I Am far greater than their assortment of so-called gods, none of whom have appeared on their behalf. The Egyptian people have newfound respect for this "god of the wilderness" who's come to town to rescue His children. So, when it's time for those children to leave here in a minute to start a new life on their own, the Egyptian people are going to give them piles of loot to help the Hebrews get a leg up from the get go. Like organizing a money tree when somebody graduates from college to give them a kick-start, only on a much bigger scale.[24]

And who else in addition to the Egyptians do you suppose has been watching this whole sequence? The Hebrews. I'll grant you, it's been a good long while since We had any direct interaction with them via Joseph, and the promises I made to Abraham have felt like distant memories. As We've noted, many understandably think I've forgotten them – both the people and the promises. Now, though, there's no question that I've remembered them both. There's also no question with regard to My ability to fulfill those promises in view of this blowout of a showdown with Egypt's purported gods. This is going to be lodged in the memory of Israel as they come against other nations in a little while – not one of them as strong as Egypt, by the way. Each of those lands is going to have their own poster god for that particular patch of territory, and I've made it crystal clear in Cairo that no "god" is going to stand in My way.

And ultimately, that's Pharaoh's problem. He's bought into the thought that "the Pharaoh is god," not unlike the Roman emperors and French kings[25] will, among others. It's the whole "power corrupts, absolute power corrupts absolutely" bugaboo. The only problem is that there is only One with absolute power, only One who is truly King, only One who is sovereign. And it ain't Baldy.

And so, to prove to Pharaoh once and for all the identity of the real King, not just of Egypt, but the true King of the World; because of his failure to

---

[23] Exodus 11:3.

[24] There's also an unmistakable whiff of self-preservation on the Egyptians' part (Exodus 12:33).

[25] No functional difference from their "Divine Right" in making themselves My equal.

respond to these ever more costly plagues and his refusal to acknowledge My sovereign Lordship or claim to My people, the final plague We bring against Egypt is of such great consequence that Pharaoh releases the Hebrews.

Now is the time for you to remember why Moses was put in that basket in the Nile eighty years earlier. That earlier pharaoh had commanded that all Hebrew baby boys be cast into the river, and they were. All of them, not just the firstborn. In a sense, then, that Pharaoh eighty years ago has chosen the final plague for this one, yet even with this act of judgment, I do not repay Egypt in full measure for the deaths of all My sons in that time. As We noted before, all of Egypt could be wiped out. In the case of the final plague, I could take all her children, or simply all her sons. That would repay Pharaoh justly for his genocidal murder of the Hebrew boys. Instead, I claim only the firstborn.

Even this has symbolism that will resonate along The Way until The End. From the very beginning, the first fruits of harvest, be they grain or livestock, have been offered to Me in a sacrifice of worship. Giving these first things to Me fosters and marks an awareness that all good things in all lives have Me as their source. The farmer may have planted and plowed the field, but Who gave him life, strength, and health to do so; or designed the seed to hold so much within it? Those new lambs and calves may be the result of romantic moonlit nights in the field, but Who made their reproductive systems work the way they do to yield fresh life? Your salary may be derived from a combination of skill, education and connections, but Who made all of those possible? In short, the first is returned to Me to acknowledge that all of it belongs to Me. Thus, when I take the firstborn of Egypt, it makes clear that all of Egypt is Mine; none of it belongs to Pharaoh. He retains his throne and life, as do his people, at My pleasure and mercy.

This is a defining moment for the Hebrews as well. They have been set aside as My people for some time now, beginning with Abraham. They have been set strongly apart from the Egyptians all these years both by their placement in Goshen and their enslavement. In these climactic weeks of confrontation, they have seen the plagues fall upon the Egyptians while the herds and crops of the Hebrews have been left untouched. My people did nothing to garner such protection in these times; the other plagues simply did not touch them. In this final plague that strikes down the firstborn of Egypt from top to bottom regardless of station, from Pharaoh's firstborn to those of stray cats, I instruct the Hebrews to take specific actions in order to shield themselves from the coming judgment.

Each family is to slaughter a lamb at twilight.[26] Its blood is to be spread on the exterior doorframe of their home. This blood will serve as a sign that death is to pass over that home and leave it untouched. The lambs must be perfect, without defect or blemish, and their blood will purchase life for those covered by it, for those homes without the sign will suffer the death of every firstborn within. In the hours following twilight, each family is to roast their lamb and eat it with unleavened bread and herbs, signs of the haste and bitterness of these hours: haste because they are soon to be run out of town, bitter both for the slavery they have endured as well as for the pain the Egyptians must endure now because of Pharaoh's pride. This simple meal will become an annual touchstone[27] for My people, a reminder of their deliverance by My hand.

At midnight, the destroyer[28] moves through the land, passing over the homes marked with the blood of a lamb, entering those that are not. The Hebrews are safe and spared; the firstborn Egyptians die in their sleep. Even this quick, painless death is a mercy in contrast to the tortured final moments of those precious boys in the Nile eighty years ago.

The night is not quiet for long, though, as the cries begin to rise up from Egyptian households, waking neighbors to make their own discoveries, as a tidal wave of anguish washes across the land, right up to the palace. Pharaoh and his officials have suffered the same loss as their countrymen, for there is not a home in Egypt without someone dead within. The king's refusal to release the Hebrews has exacted a severe cost, enough to finally soften his pride and move him to free My people. He calls Moses and Aaron to the palace in the middle of the night, and in contrast of his "negotiated freedom" offers made in response to more recent plagues, he capitulates fully this time, telling the brothers to leave and take all the Hebrews (not just the men) with all their flocks and herds (not just enough animals for a few sacrifices) and, "Get out of Egypt and go worship Yahveh! And Moses, bless me on your way out!"[29]

There it is, release *and* acknowledgement of My existence. While Baldy isn't asking Moses to ask Me to bless him, asking My prophet for a blessing amounts to pretty much the same thing. Pharaoh finally acknowledges there

---

[26] Exodus 12:21–28.
[27] Exodus 12:16–20.
[28] Exodus 12:23, often referred to as "the angel of death" in your habitat.
[29] Exodus 12:29–32.

is something in Egypt – or someOne – greater than him. And just like that, everything changes.

Pharaoh's finally ready for the Hebrews to leave. The Hebrews, certainly, are ready to leave. The Egyptian people are more than ready for them to leave, and in a hurry. They're afraid that every last Egyptian will die if the Hebrews stay around even a minute longer. So sympathetic with the Hebrews have the Egyptian people become (and so very much wanting them to get out and stay out), that when the Israelites ask their Egyptian "hosts" for clothes (of which the Hebrews have few), silver and gold (of which the Hebrews have none), the Egyptians load the suddenly former slaves down with heaps of booty, literally packing their bags for them, just as We predicted.[30]

And so the final swarm is that of the Hebrews as they leave their unpleasant Egyptian incubator, and their numbers have so swollen that the Israelites far outnumber the Egyptians; so this is quite a parade heading out of Egypt. Remember, Israel has got its own flocks – descended from those brought in by Joseph's brothers just as the humans have descended from those shepherds – and the Hebrews' animals have been untouched by the three plagues that laid the Egyptians' protein in the dust (livestock, hail, and finally, the few remaining firstborn). Thus, outnumbering the thousands upon thousands of departing humans, even greater swarms of flocks and herds accompany the Hebrews, leaving a trail of organic fertilizer in their wake. Pharaoh won't need to follow breadcrumbs to find these people after they leave.

In all the cacophony of kids (human and goat), cattle, sheep and shouts of joy, I have Moses quiet the people and do what every good leader does in momentous moments like this. This is a defining moment in all of history, so it's a good time for a speech. It is vital that what is happening right now be remembered, and so while the dust of Egypt is still on their sandals, Moses sets the annual observance of a ceremonial reenactment of all that's gone on, of all that I have done with My mighty hand to set Israel free. I know you humans too well to think that these things will not fade from memory as years of bounty wash over them unless a strong cadence of reminder is put in place. Now's the perfect moment to place it; here in the midst of deliverance as the Hebrews are about to cross the border out of Egypt into a new reality. And so, just as each family sacrificed a lamb so that that lamb's blood would mark the redemption of that household's firstborn from death,

---

[30] Exodus 12:33–36.

in coming years, each family will sacrifice another lamb to remember how Israel's freedom came at the high cost of Egypt's firstborn.

Thus, in addition to setting this reminder for My people in Moses' farewell speech, I also lay My claim to all the firstborn of Israel, human or animal, with all the assertion of possession and Kingship over the entire nation that claim carries with it. The firstborn humans have been consecrated to Me by the blood of their Passover lambs (as well as by the lives of their precious Egyptian counterparts), and now the firstborn of the flocks and herds are sacrificed to Me as well. This conveys not simply that all the firstborn of Israel belong to Me, but that every life in the nation is Mine. (We will have a great deal more to say about sacrifice once We have time to set up a formal system with Moses and Our people, but We Are in a bit of a hurry to get everybody out of Dodge just now while still marking this moment poignant with the sacredness of the consecrating sacrifice of the firstborn.)[31]

Now, if you look at a map, you can see it's a pretty short trip from Egypt to the specific land I've been promising Abraham, Isaac, Jacob and their swarming offspring. To head straight there, though, would require going right through the Philistines, Egypt's annoyingly military neighbors to the northeast.[32] The Hebrews have been living a life of bone-crushing hardship for quite some time, though, so We intend to give them some rest and relaxation before the drama ramps up again.[33] Plus, you already know We have one more wonder up Our sleeve before Our Egyptian exchange comes to a close.

Moses leads the people south, or rather, I do. I form a pillar of cloud just to the south of the gathered Hebrews, near where Moses has been speaking. Most of your imaginations are coming up with something that looks like a white tornado, thanks in large part to your movies, but that's not quite it. It doesn't actually matter what it looks like, other than these facts: It's not a naturally occurring phenomenon, it's a manifestation of My presence; and Moses and the people are far less concerned with "How is He doing that" than they are giddy with the clear evidence that "Yahveh is with us, and He Is on the move." I'll shift the pillar from cloud by day to fire at night as a giant nightlight for everyone, visible from space to those of Us with a larger perspective.

---

[31] Exodus 12:43–13:16 for the full account, Exodus 13:11–16 for Moses' speech. Note that in My repeated faithfulness to and through him in all the previous episodes Moses has fully found his voice.

[32] Know why they're so military? They're Egypt's neighbors.

[33] Exodus 13:17–22.

Then comes the big climax you've all been waiting for. I lead the Israelites to a picturesque spot beside the sea. Meanwhile, back at the palace, the shock and haze of the final plague have lifted, and Pharaoh's awakened to the sound of silence across the land. No Hebrews making bricks, cutting stone, setting pylons, doing dishes, cooking breakfast, watching children, washing laundry, scrubbing floors, nor any of the other myriad menial or substantial tasks that had been their lot as Egypt's slaves. Even his advisors, the ones who'd urged their king to release the Hebrews in order to escape the plagues, change their tune when they realize they'll have to do their own everything now. "What have we done? We have let the Israelites go and have lost their services!"[34] So in a Memphis minute, Pharaoh and six hundred of his best chariots are in hot pursuit[35] of the boldly departed slaves.

Which brings about some of Our favorite sarcasm in The Owner's Manual. When My people see Pharaoh headed in their general direction, they unload on Moses, "Was it because there were no graves in Egypt that you brought us to the desert to die?" They moan that continued life as a slave would have better than death with a view of the seashore. Nice, right? As if the past ten episodes never happened. They've got no faith, these people. Moses tells them so, instructing them not to panic. Just hang tight and see what happens. With the most important part: "The LORD[36] will fight for you; you need only to be still."[37]

Write that one down in your journal, friend. This is another archetypal moment in Our life with humanity, a theme that will be repeated[38] over and over in all kinds of circumstances. I've said it before, and I'll say it again: If I have put you in a circumstance, I will do what it takes to get you out of it. If I have asked you to do something, I will be there to help you do it. Who's got the power? I do. I will fight for you; you only need to keep still.

All the people have to do is be a little patient while I work. I move My pillar to block the chariots from getting through, and here's a fun detail about that night – the side of the pillar facing the Hebrews is bright with light, while the opposite side's not only dark, but it spreads a felt darkness (not made with the craft material, but perceived with the sense of touch)

---

[34] Exodus 14:5.
[35] Long before Roscoe P. Coltrane was ever dreamed of.
[36] My Name, *YHVH,* is in the original Hebrew text here, not *ADONAI,* the Hebrew word for Lord.
[37] Exodus 14:10–14.
[38] Psalm 46:10!

over Egypt's camp, a lot like that ninth plague had done. Throw in one of My own special forces angels to boot, and Pharaoh and his strike force aren't going anywhere.[39]

Then it happens, but not like you think. Yes, Moses raises his staff and stretches out his hand over the sea, but this is no Universal Studios tour. I haven't got secret hydraulic walls embedded in the sea bottom, and it doesn't happen in the wink of an eye. If you look at the biblical text, you'll see old Moses is out there all night, and I drive the sea back and divide the waters with a strong east wind, leaving a wall of water *on each side*. Tuck that last bit in for nearby use.

Now, some fools have said, "You see! It says right here this wasn't a miracle! Just a strong wind blowing the water away!" These people have neither looked at a meteorology textbook nor experienced even a weak hurricane. Yes, there are winds that are strong enough to move large masses of water, but not in two opposing directions, pal, as in a wall of water *on both sides.* (See?) Let's say, though, that it's just a one-direction wind for the sake of argument. A wind strong enough to move and hold back that amount of water is going to have to be both very powerful *and* last a good long while. A huge gust can move literally tons of water, but a gust doesn't hold them back; the very strong water-moving wind would have to be sustained. So if you're trying to limit this event strictly to a naturally-occurring phenomenon, then record-breaking hurricane force winds are going to be in order. Those just might move and hold back the water.

Have you detected the problems with this scenario? First and foremost, while every great while there's a rare tornado in Egypt, even a big one wouldn't do the trick because those don't remain even remotely stationary, which would be necessary to make the narrative work. The storms that could theoretically move this amount of water - hurricanes, typhoons, or tropical cyclones – do not occur in Egypt. Ever. Let's say they did though. Well, there's another instant problem. How on earth is anyone going to walk anywhere in 190 mph winds? As soon as it lets up, the water comes back, so people are going to have to be walking directly through and even across category five hurricane force winds that are pushing and holding the water back to (just one) side. You can see the futility of this thinking. The Hebrews wouldn't be able to take a single theoretical step. They and all their sheep, goats and assorted paraphernalia would be blown into the next time zone.

---

[39] Honestly, if you're tracking with the text, just read Exodus 14:19–31, the rest of the chapter.

So, listen up here, friend. As We go through some of Our miraculous interactions with the human race, keep this moment in mind. As We mentioned with the earlier plagues, there will be times We in some way use the nature We created to bring about a desired outcome. You'll see, however, that just as in the case of Our parting the sea, it's always in a way that far surpasses a freak coincidental event at just the precisely right time. Sure, a wind may come along now and then (and more often now than in those days) that can pile up a whole lot of water, but good luck leading a nation through that wind as you walk leisurely across a mucky sea bottom littered with gasping starfish, urchins, and other unfortunate bottom stickers.

Wait a minute, now. How does that whole dry land thing happen overnight too if this is all a natural occurrence? Sure, steady wind would dry the exposed surface, but deep enough into the soggy strata to the point of being able to fully support the weight of all the herds, flocks, and feet of the fleeing nation? Not gonna happen. I must be the one doing it after all. Sure seems to make the most sense.

Thank Me, Moses and Israel certainly think I Am the one doing it all, and they head out on the highway through the sea. As We've described, this is a whole lot of people and animals, so it takes a good while even though they are highly motivated to travel as quickly as possible. I've got perfect timing (all the time), and lift My restrictions on the Egyptian pursuers so they will not catch up with the scrambling Hebrews in spite of the speed of Pharaoh's charioteers. "Coincidentally," their wheels happen to jam at just the worst time too, slowing them up in their chase. [40] Those same Egyptian advisors that saw My hand in the plagues see it again as so many chariots are waylaid in their ride through the sea, but too late. As the final Hebrew steps onto the other side, Moses stretches out his hand over the sea, and it returns to its normal state. And as the waters close forever over the fleeing chariots of Pharaoh, the decades-past drowning of all Our baby boys is fully avenged, and the slavery of My people to Egypt comes to a final close.

Before We close this chapter, though, let Us process and apply a bit of this swath of divine-human/human-human interaction that's just gone past. Like We said earlier, in addition to being a nail-biting, edge-of-your-seat thriller of an action sequence, this whole kit and caboodle of Israel and Egypt serves as another archetype that functions on levels both individual (as in applying concretely right now to your life – yep, your life right there in

---

[40] Another detail missed in movies (Exodus 14:24–25).

Tucumcari, Keokuk, Calabash, Oconomowoc, or wherever you call home) and universal (as in the human race in its general entirety).

I'm guessing that not many of you have statues of ancient Egyptian gods enshrined in your living room to which you pray or at which you aim your worship. Some of you may have statues that represent Us towards which you do such things, in which case I refer you to the "graven image" section of the next volume. At any rate, with or without the use of statuary, idolatry is alive and well today, My friend, and it's more destructively powerful and insidious than it was in the greatest glory days of Amun-Ra.

You see, an idol doesn't have to be a formal god or deity.[41] Think about those Egyptian "gods." They were each in charge of something – fertility, health, bugs, whatever. So an idol can be anything that's not Me that you put "in charge" of part (or all) of your life. It's a matter of allegiance, really. A matter of what is driving you – the thing that is the prime mover in your life that motivates you at your core; again, *if* that prime mover and motivator is not Me. An idol is whatever is in charge of your heart – that which is on the throne of your heart – whatever determines how you define that which is good, important, worth sacrificing for, and a whole cascade of determinations that trickle down to the tiniest details of your life.

People put all manner of things on the thrones of their hearts. Obviously, I Am your optimal "option." That's how you're designed. I Am the perfect fit. No other god nor idol will come even close to working like the Original Equipment Manufacturer Himself. Just now in Our story, the Hebrews are in the process of learning that there is only one God, that He's Me, and it is only I that deserve the allegiance of their hearts. There's no need to departmentalize like the Egyptians do – one god for this, another for that. I'm your one stop God and heart-throne-filler. As I pick off each of those Egyptian deities and beat them in each of their allegedly strong suits, I make it clear that I Am sovereign over all things, all departments of life and living, and that there's no need to look any further than Moi when seeking a target for your heart's allegiance.

There are still idols out there, though. Oh, you can pat yourself on the back for being too highly evolved to fall for a falcon-headed god sailing the sun across the sky every day. You've got the whole How the Natural Universe Works thing down, or at least you think so.[42] There are other idols, though,

---

[41] Or a thentofore unknown yet talented singer vaulted to stardom on a television program.
[42] Indeed, some of you have made the universe itself an idol, thanking it for this and that, when I Am the maker of universes and the rightful target of your thanks. You may think you're being politically correct; you're also being idolatrous.

that determine your steps. Dare I say it? Idols that dictate your choices and steps, idols that drive your thoughts and goals just as surely as Amun, Anubis, Heket and Ra – or rather, as surely as the *thought* of these – drove the Egyptians' daily life and conduct.

What is it you want more than anything else in the world? If it's not Me, there's a very good chance it's an idol on your heart's throne, calling the shots whether you know it or not. Think about it. What drives you? What are you going after with your life? Money? Pleasure? Relationship? Children? Security? Comfort? Entertainment? Career? Influence? I like all of them. I made all of them. Even though most of these things could be described as an experience, they are all still created things. Created by Me. Your heart is designed for only one thing to fit well in the throne slot – Me. Put something else there, even something good like your family or feeling secure, and it will fail you. Because it's not Me. When the times of trial come along, those things will let you down because they don't have the power to carry you through the tough times. I do. Trust in money as your idol, and it will surely betray you whether you run out of it or have more than you need. Everyone who says they'd like to give it a try and gets the chance can tell you so. And kids? I love them! I made them! But if they *are* your life, when they grow up and leave (trust Me, that's what's supposed to happen), you're going to feel like your anchor's been cut loose. Same with every other option that's not Me.

Look back at the plagues now. Who showed up to deal with them? The idols whose territory they were in? Nope. Just big ole Me. Crisis will come in your life, friend – there are too many people on the planet making poor choices for anyone to escape hardship and crisis. When it comes, it'll be bigger than your idol can handle. Here's what you do. Call on Me. I'll get you through.

Now, I've had plenty of experience with folks who've just picked up the Godphone to call Me in emergencies, then forgotten Me once things got back to "normal," like I'm some kind of Gotham City superhero. Like I'm ready to fix things when they're broken, then happy to let you go on your merry way once the crisis is over. Well, friend, let Me tell you this. I'm no genie in a bottle, lucky rabbit's foot, get-out-of-jail-free card, nor whatever other entity you might imagine you have at your beck and call solely for times of need. I Am the Sovereign Lord of All that Is. I will not be put in your back pocket to be pulled out merely when you've gotten yourself in a pickle. I deserve far more than Panic Button Status in your life. I deserve the entire throne of your heart. Put Me there, friend, and not only will We handle crises together, but all the good stuff will be all the sweeter in its rightful place. And it all works so much better when you enthrone Me in times of measured reflection and conviction like this instead of on your deathbed or in moments in which you feel like you're headed straight for it. Put Me on the throne of your heart now, and I Am already there when trouble comes.

Okay, so We've covered modern idolatry – at least as much as We're going to. Honestly, it's a lifelong struggle for most folks, but it's all so much easier when I'm invited to the party ahead of time. Before We move Our narrative on, just two more quick things. First, take a quick look at Pharaoh. Sure, he worships a plethora of idols like the rest of his culture, but he has an extra feature that many of you struggle with as well. If he's nothing else, the king of Egypt is certainly Mr. I Can Handle This. This guy is so full and sure of himself that he imagines himself My equal, or better. Even as the stakes are raised and the consequences mount up, the prideful hardness of his heart won't let him recognize the fact that he is wrong in his estimation of Me and of himself. You know somebody just like this guy.[43] There's no convincing this fellow there's anything out there greater than himself.

Now, you may not be as blatant as the bald king is in his swagger, but there are moments when you think to yourself, "I've got this, God," for whatever reason. You think I'll complicate the situation with the inconvenience of ethics. You simply want to have things your way for a change. You like the feeling of control and fancy the driver's seat. Be warned, friend. This attitude will eventually come back around and bite you in the consequences, and those consequences will generally be paired with your level of arrogance, as Pharaoh's are.

Finally, before We leave Egypt behind, I want to again underscore the fact that Israel's journey serves as a template for what's going on even now in your life and that of all humanity. On its simplest level, there's a lot to identify with. As We've striven to establish from the beginning, the situation in which you find yourself is not as was intended. You were purposed for a much better life on every level. Instead, you're being held captive in an existence that seems at times to hold sorrow, pain, and cruelty at every turn. I assure you, I have heard your cries, though I know it may not seem to be the case. However, just as I prepared and sent Moses at just the right time to deliver My people, your Deliverer is ready and waiting for My call. And He will come at just the right time, and you shall be free. Free beyond your wildest dreams, friend.

---

[43] Anybody remember Arthur Fonzarelli?

Meanwhile, back at the ranch, or at least on the other side of the sea and finally free from Egypt, the Hebrews have a hoedown with Moses and his sister Miriam supplying the music[44] in the form of praise to Me for getting everybody out safe and sound. Then it's time to head to "My" mountain. Not to beat a deceased equine, but remember, I'm working with these folks where they are, and they've still got a geographically localized view of deity. As far as they're concerned, Moses knows where to find Me – that mountain on which he and I had Our sandals-off chat at the beginning of the chapter. So he's taking them there to rendezvous with Me for what they'll perceive to be their first time in My presence.

Now, ask Heraclitus about change, and he'll tell you it's the only constant in human experience. Ask the humans with whom you're acquainted how they like change, and they won't. Even change for the better is hard to take for people, with an obvious case in point in this large crew of Hebrews who've just been liberated from centuries of slavery. Granted, they're having to cross a good stretch of desert to get out to My mountain, but they still haven't learned what it means for Me to have their back. Once they run out of the food they'd packed, the Israelites start in with the complaints. "We were surrounded by potfuls of meat and all the bread we could eat back in Egypt. We'd rather have died as slaves with full bellies than starve to death free like this."[45]

Tsk, tsk, tsk, tsk, tsk.[46] Take a lesson from these people, will you? (That *is* the point of their being both in The Owner's Manual as well as in the tome you're surveying.) Exactly which problem have I not handled up to this point? Naturally, I may have handled them in times and ways least expected, but if you haven't figured out that My ways aren't exactly yours yet, I think you've been doing a little too much multitasking while reading this book, friend. Stop checking your email every other paragraph and pay better attention.

Because, before I can get them to the mountain, My children have to learn a couple more lessons. Let's actually make it three for now. First, in many ways, freedom holds far greater challenge and requires far more faith than slavery. Since you like to multitask so much, go ahead and extrapolate that sentence into your own life right away. Freedom holds far greater challenge and requires far more faith than slavery. The overriding aspect to being enslaved is that all your choices are made for you. With freedom

---

[44] See Exodus 15.

[45] We Are in Exodus 16 now.

[46] You know what that spells, right? For full effect, shake your head slowly from side to side while you do it.

comes a much broader menu of options from which to choose along with the monumental challenge of getting to – and having to – think for yourself. Not just in terms of "What'll I have for breakfast?" but also in terms of "What'll I do with my life?" Just ask, and I'll be happy to give you a hand with both.

Which is the second lesson the Hebrews learn. I make sure they have enough food to live on. Most of you don't know the meaning of the word "hunger" other than the self-induced form you've experienced either on purpose or as a result of somebody's poor planning. It's a different case with these folks. They are headed into a wilderness devoid of grocery, restaurant, or deli; running out of supplies is of rightful concern. However, instead of making a simple, polite request for something to eat, they go straight to complaining. As such, they are mighty lucky I don't act like most of your parents at this juncture. Most of your folks wouldn't respond to a whiny demand from you and would hold out until you asked for something nicely. However, I know My Hebrew children still have a great deal to learn, including better manners, so in spite of their recalcitrant attitude and the fact that all they do is grumble at Me instead of requesting My help, I go ahead and accept their complaint as the only way they know how to ask for food at this point. If I were to wait until they say "please" before taking care of them, they'd be nothing but sun-bleached desert bones in no time.

Now, note the unexpected way in which I satisfy their hunger. They're not reduced to living off snakes, scorpions, and desert rats. I bestow upon them savory meat – quail, no less. An ample number of the plump birdies pretty much fly into camp at sunset every night. Then, in the morning: bread from heaven, friend. You've heard of it, right? This is where manna enters the story. Every morning when Israel wakes up, the surrounding desert is covered with it. I'm not giving up My recipe for manna just yet, but I do want to dispel all the theories that is something that would've happened without My intervention. This is not sap or bug poop, people. It's bread. And the Israelites are instructed to gather what they need for the day; no more, no less.

Which brings Us to the third and final lesson On The Way to the mountain. This lesson actually establishes a theme that We will very much underscore in Our mountain time with the people as well, but this is their first acquaintance with it. It's something you may not be familiar with on a personal level either, given the current situation in your habitat. My guess is that you've heard about this concept, but never really experienced it. As slaves, the Hebrews had not been introduced to it either, but as you'll see, I Am quite certain that this is a fundamental need for each one of you on a multitude of levels. After such a buildup, what could this important lesson possibly be? (Drumroll, please.) Brace yourself. Here it is: R. E. S. T. You need it, more than you know. Even though Aretha never sang about it.

Now, I don't come right out and tell this to the Hebrews straight like that, that they really need rest. Well, I kind of tell them, but on a bit of a casual level, if I may put it that way. You see, I want them to learn this lesson deeply, so I help them discover it on their own. Their need for rest – and My desire for that rest – is embedded in My instructions about their groceries. On all days, they're only to gather enough for that day. Nothing better than fresh anything, right? However, in seeming contradiction to this mandate, I advise them to collect a double portion on the sixth day, in order that *they can rest* on the seventh and not worry about a single thing all the way down to fixing supper.

To make sure they learn the lesson, there's a bit of reinforcement built in, especially to the manna. You know they're only to collect enough for that day each day most days, but did I mention that they're also to finish it all by the day's end and not keep any overnight? Know what happens if they don't listen and hold some until the next day? The sweet manna stinks to high heaven and is riddled with maggots as a bonus. Not exactly how you want to be getting your protein, especially with the load of juicy dark meat flying in that night. However, on the seventh day, when I've told them to collect twice as much the day before and keep half of it overnight, the holdover manna smells as sweet as honey the next morning, with not a larva in sight.

And the point of it all is how serious I Am about this rest thing. Which We'll get to, as I said, but since it's going to be such a big deal, and since it's something you get around to once a year if you're lucky, I really want to point out this exposition of the restful theme – like that flute solo My boy Edvard Grieg and I came up with[47] – here in its proper place.

And speaking of proper places, suffice it to say that, with their bellies full of meat and bread (and miraculous water here and there along the way when necessary), Moses and I finally get the new nation to the foot of My mountain so We can begin Our new chapter of life with them. The Abraplan, the working out of which is going to bring about the rescue of all humanity, is about to move to another level entirely. This requires not just a new chapter, but a new volume. Meet you there.

---

[47] That would be the "Morgenstemning" (literally and appropriately, "morning mood") theme in the Prelude to Act IV of *Peer Gynt*. You know it, but didn't know that's where We put it.

www.ingramcontent.com/pod-product-compliance
Lightning Source LLC
Chambersburg PA
CBHW032047090426
42744CB00004B/108